MW00635406

Jim Beam® Figural Bottles

An Unauthorized Collector's Guide

Molly Higgins

Schiffer Publishing Ltd

4880 Lower Valley Road, Atglen, PA 19310 USA

Dedication

To Mouschi, Fritz, Mitsu, and Pongo—my four-footed brigade.

DISCLAIMER
The text and products pictured in this book are from various private collectors. This book is not sponsored, endorsed, or otherwise affiliated with with any of the companies whose products are represented herein. They include James B. Beam Distilling Company, and Regal China, and Wade Ceramics, Ltd. This book is derived from the author's private research.

Revised 2nd Edition
Copyright © 2005 by Schiffer Publishing, Ltd.
Library of Congress Control Number: 2004113300

All rights reserved. No part of this work may be reproduced or used in any form or by any means—graphic, electronic, or mechanical, including photocopying or information storage and retrieval systems—without written permission from the publisher.
The scanning, uploading and distribution of this book or any part thereof via the Internet or via any other means without the permission of the publisher is illegal and punishable by law. Please purchase only authorized editions and do not participate in or encourage the electronic piracy of copyrighted materials.
"Schiffer," "Schiffer Publishing Ltd. & Design," and the "Design of pen and ink well" are registered trademarks of Schiffer Publishing Ltd.

Book Design by Anne Davidsen
Photography by Molly Higgins
Type set in OzHandicraft/Korinna

ISBN: 0-7643-2181-1
Printed in China
1 2 3 4

Published by Schiffer Publishing Ltd.
4880 Lower Valley Road
Atglen, PA 19310
Phone: (610) 593-1777; Fax: (610) 593-2002
E-mail: Info@schifferbooks.com

For the largest selection of fine reference books on this and related subjects, please visit our web site at
www.schifferbooks.com
We are always looking for people to write books on new and related subjects. If you have an idea for a book please contact us at the above address.

This book may be purchased from the publisher.
Include $3.95 for shipping.
Please try your bookstore first.
You may write for a free catalog.

In Europe, Schiffer books are distributed by
Bushwood Books
6 Marksbury Ave.
Kew Gardens
Surrey TW9 4JF England
Phone: 44 (0) 20 8392-8585; Fax: 44 (0) 20 8392-9876
E-mail: info@bushwoodbooks.co.uk
Free postage in the U.K., Europe; air mail at cost.

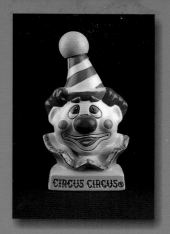

Jim Beam Figural Bottles

An Unauthorized Collector's Guide

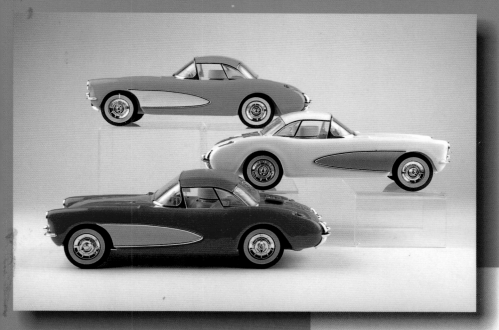

Molly Higgins

2 edition

Revised **2nd** *Edition*

A Schiffer Book for Collectors   With Price Guide

About the Author

Molly Higgins is a writer and editor living on a farm in southeastern Pennsylvania. She loves art, music, coxing for her crew team, and all things automotive.

Table of Contents

Acknowledgements

This book could never have been written were it not for the help of many people. Bill and Dollie Bostic welcomed us into their home in gorgeous Ruidoso, New Mexico to photograph their enormous and beautifully organized collection.

Thanks to:

Billy the Kid Beamers Club of New Mexico for their warm introduction to the fellowship of Beam bottle collectors.

Tina Skinner, who set this project in motion and played a vital role in the photo shoot.

Art and Judy Turner (right), who offered a great deal of insight and assistance. The Turners have been bottle collectors and dealers for 25 years; their business, Homestead Collectables, is in Mill Hall, Pennsylvania. They are currently the Bottle Show Chairpersons for the International Association of Jim Beam Bottle and Specialties Clubs. You can reach them at:

Homestead Collectables
P.O. Box 173
Mill Hall, PA 17751
E-mail: jturner@kcnet.org
Website: www.homesteadcollectables.com

The Evergreen Club of Washington state, for maintaining such an excellent website. (www.beamclub.com). Featuring an auction, a message board, a huge gallery, and all kinds of Beam bottle information, this is the premier website for bottle collectors.

Introduction

Welcome Beamers!

Welcome to the wonderful world of Jim Beam decanter collecting. These elaborate figural bottles were made in ceramic or glass and sold in liquor stores. They became so much more than just a fancy package for high-quality Jim Beam liquors; hundreds of different designs were produced with collectors in mind from the 1940s to the present.

The great majority of bottles featured in this book were produced by the Regal China Company. Regal began around 1940 on the outskirts of Chicago, Illinois. Herman Kravitz and his assistant Catherine Miller worked to expand the small company to become a major supplier of ceramic components, primarily bases for lamps.

Meanwhile, Martin Lewin, of the James B. Beam Distilling Company, was exploring new, creative packaging that would make Jim Beam products more eye-catching and suitable to give as gifts. Around Christmas of 1953, the company released a glass cocktail shaker, which was immensely popular.

By 1955, Lewin was still searching for attractive packaging solutions to move surplus liquor, and ceramic bottles were another possibility; he approached the Regal China company. The first bottle Regal designer Dave Nissen designed for Beam was the White China Ashtray. The decanter was introduced on the market with some skepticism, although it sold with great success. Nissen continued on to design hundreds of decanters in the years that followed. The White Ashtray began the wonderful alliance of Jim Beam and Regal China, one that lasted nearly forty years.

Regal China bottles are clearly marked on the bottom. The name "C. Miller" (for Catherine Miller, artistic visionary for Regal China) was copyrighted and incorporated into the stamp as a symbol of quality.

On the secondary market, bottles range in price from a couple of dollars into the hundreds, and occasionally even the thousands. They can be found anywhere, including flea markets, garage sales, Internet auctions, as well as Beam club functions and conventions.

The decanter designs are fascinating, as they were made to celebrate many subject areas. Through them, the Beamer (which is the affectionate nickname for a Beam bottle collector) will learn about art, automobiles, geography, history, sports, folklore, politics, and much more. The bottles also reflect a great deal about the traditions of Beam bottle collecting, including clubs, conventions, and the leaders that have made the field what it is today.

Using This Guide

Jim Beam Decanters each belong to a specific series, which can be very helpful to the collector. It's not always so simple; sometimes two decanters that look very similar belong to different series.

In order to make identification a little easier, the decanters in this guide have been divided into three sections: ceramic, glass, and vehicles. Within these categories, the bottles have been sorted by series, and are listed chronologically within each series.

For the most part, the decanters appear with their proper series. However, some decanters are very close, if not identical, in appearance, and often these bottles have been grouped together in the photographs to illustrate subtle differences. The clearest example of this is with the vehicle-shaped decanters. For example, Angelo's Liquors offered a number of Jim Beam vehicle decanters. While the Angelo's bottles are a part of the Customer Specialty series, many of these bottles appear in this book with the Wheel Series. These "cross-over" bottles have all been cross-referenced to eliminate any confusion.

We have covered a large assortment of decanters, although this book is not intended to be complete. I welcome information from other collectors in hopes of bigger and better future editions!

Pricing Decanters

The decanters pictured in this book all appear with price estimates in the captions. These prices come from several sources, including books, auctions, and collectors. Of course, condition plays a vital role in determining the value of any item on the secondary market, so be certain to investigate the item fully. Prices can vary widely depending on both buyer and seller, and ultimately these decanters are only worth what you are willing to pay for them.

Care of Your Decanters

Usually, collectible items are most valuable in a pristene, unopened, mint-in-package state. It's a little different for ceramic decanters. While it might seem that an unopened bottle with an unbroken tax stamp, full of aging whiskey, might hold a higher value than an empty one, this is not the case. *Decanters on the collector's market need to be empty.* There are a number of reasons for this.

First, it's doubtful that you as a decanter collector will want to get a liquor license, but that's what you're going to need if you want to sell full bottles without breaking the law. Second, as the cork ages, it dries out and cracks, which allows oxygen into the bottle and ruins the contents. The alcohol will not age in the bottle like it did in the barrel, so if you plan to drink it, don't wait. Third, as ceramic bottles expand and contract with changes in temperature, hairline cracks in the glaze (called crazing) will form. Liquor left in the bottle will cause further corrosion, which could very possibly lead to bigger cracks and leaking. Fourth, full bottles are more trouble to store than empty ones; not only does alcohol pose a great fire hazard, but full bottles weigh about two pounds more—why strain your shelves with the added weight of undrinkable whiskey?

Other than making sure the bottle is empty, there's not a whole lot you need to do. A dab of petroleum jelly rubbed into the cork from time to time will keep it from drying out—many bottles have hard-to-replace ceramic tops, so it's a good idea to make sure the cork stays in good shape. An occasional dusting or even a washing with warm soapy water (be sure to avoid any labels) will keep the bottle looking its best. Most Beam decanters have fired-on color, which will not fade under scrubbing. Some decanters do have some unfired paint, so be on the lookout! If you aren't certain, be sure to test a small, inconspicuous area first.

The Collectors' Community

Few fields can boast the kind of community of collectors that Beamers share. There are thousands of long-time collectors, and newcomers are always welcome. Clubs have formed throughout the United States and the world, united through the International Association of Jim Beam Bottle & Specialties Clubs (IAJBB&SC). The association organizes their legendary annual convention, and there are several other gatherings at both the district and club levels year round—often offering limited edition bottles! To find out more about the IAJBB&SC, and the club nearest you, contact:

International Association of Jim Beam Bottle and
Specialty Clubs
2015 Burlington Avenue
Kewanee, IL 61443

Ceramic Decanters

Armed Forces Series

1970-1984

Germany, 1970. Map of
country on back. $5-10

Germany, Hansel and Gretel,
1972. "Munchen" on back. $5-10

Submarine Redfin, 1970. "Operation Redfin" on back. $5-10

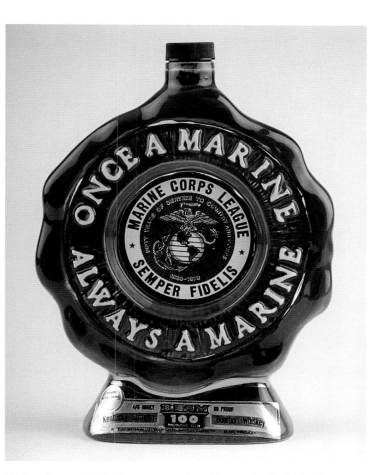

Short Timer, 1975. $25-30

Marine Corps, 1975. Monument at Iwo Jima on back. $40-45

101st Airborne,
1977. $10-15

Marine "Devil Dog", 1979. $40-45

D-Day, 1984. $18-22

Canteen, 1980. $15-20

Boots and Helmet, 1984. Very collectible among Army personnel
and collectors. $25-35

Beam Award Series

1972-1981

Two '34 Ford salesman awards were produced for this series, in black and yellow, that are not pictured here. $700-800, $500-600

Red Coat fox, 1973. Very few of these were produced—approximately 40. They were given to distillery employees as incentive awards. Decanter, $700. The smaller fox is Renard, the Royal Doulton figurine that inspired the design of Rennie, the smart-looking mascot who has made so many Beam decanter appearances. $45-50.

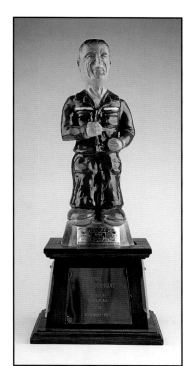

Colonel Oliphant was the largest purchaser of Jim Beam Decanters for the Army PX's. When he retired in 1974, this decanter was made in his honor. This is a rare bottle. $300+

Sam Baer donkey, 1972. Presented to the 44 people in attendance at his retirement party from the Jim Beam Distilling Company. $1,800

Millionth Barrel Bottle, 1980. Bottle #64. Signed on the back by Beam presidents J.J. McShane and Barry Berish. $400+

Beam Collection
1979-1981

Screech Owl, red and grey, 1979. $18-22

Giant Panda, 1980. $15-20

Jaguar, 1981. $27-32

Blue Goose, 1979. $8-12.
Snow Goose, 1979. $12-15

Centennial Series

1960-1985

One member of this series not appearing here is the Grand Canyon bottle, 1969.

St. Louis Arch: 1964, $15-20. 1965-66, $12-17. 1967-68, $10-15.

Civil War bottles, 1961. North, $20-25. South, $28-33.

Santa Fe, 1960. "Land of Enchantment" with Indian potter on back. $85-90

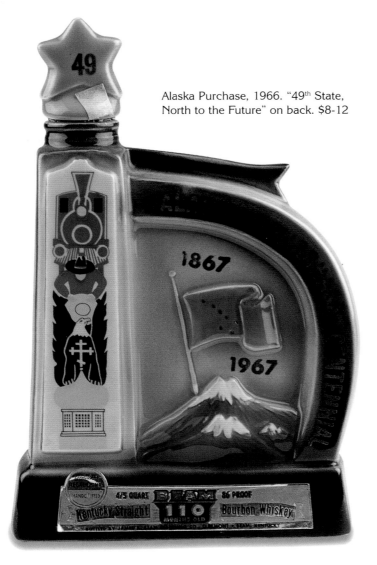

Alaska Purchase, 1966. "49th State, North to the Future" on back. $8-12

Antioch, 1967. "Diamond Jubilee" on the back. With foam arrow, $8-10. Without arrow, $4-7.

San Diego, 1968. Shown in three color variations. Picture of missionaries on back. $2-7

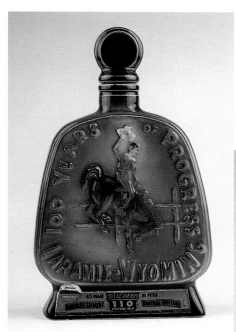

Laramie, Wyoming, 1968. "Centennial Jubilee" on back. $5-10

Cheyenne Centennial, 1967. "Cheyenne Wyoming, 1867-1967" on back. $5-10

Reno, 1968. "Reno 100 Years" on back. $5-10

Lombard Lilac Festival, 1969. Two variations in color shown on stoppers. $5-10

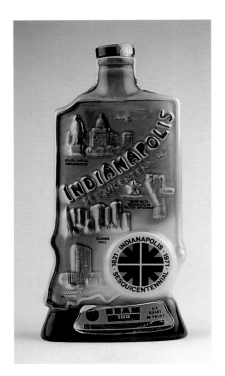

Indianapolis Sesquicentennial, 1971.
Short history on back. $5-10

Dodge City, Boot Hill, 1972. Short history
on back. $8-12

Yellowstone Park, 1972. $5-10

Colorado Springs Centennial 100 bottle.
"Pike's Peak" and landscape on back, $8-12.
Colorado Centennial, 1976, $8-12.

Key West, 1972. History of the island on back. $5-10

Statue of Liberty, 1975. "Give me your tired..."
on back. $20-25

Reidsville, 1973. "City of Reidsville, North Carolina,
Centennial" on back. $8-12

New Mexico Bicentennial, 1976.
"A cultural mosaic" on back. $8-12

Hawaii 200th, 1978. $15-20

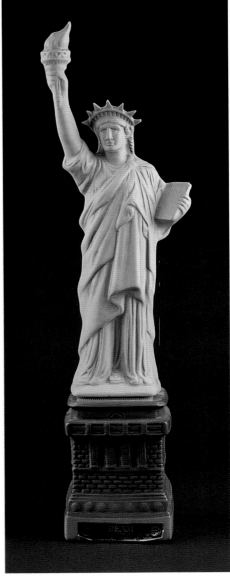

Above: Statue of Liberty, 1985. "Give me
your tired..." on back. $20-30

Left: Washington State Bicentennial, 1976.
$13-18

Club Series

1967-1983

The first Beam collectors' club was formed in 1966 in Berkely, California, with sixteen members. A year later, the club boasted one hundred members and other clubs were forming nationwide. In 1971, the first convention was held for the National Association of Jim Beam Bottle and Specialty Clubs, which unified clubs nationwide for a combined total of 19,000 members. By 1973, the National Association became the International Association, to welcome several other clubs that were springing up overseas.

Today, the IAJBB&SC consists of about 135 regional clubs spread throughout twelve districts worldwide.

Not appearing in this section is the Evergreen Club bottle, 1974.

Blue coat fox, 1967, $55-60. Gold coat fox, 1969, $250-300. Green coat fox (Trophy series), 1965-67, $12-17.

Silver President's Achievement Award, 1980. White coat fox, 1969, $20-25. Queen Mary gold coat fox, 1969, $250-300.

19

Hawaii Aloha Club, 1971 (right). Pictured with a nearly identical bottle issued for the Regal China series (left). The club bottle has a club medallion on the bottle; the Regal bottle reads "King Kamehamea" near the bottom.

Rocky Mountain Club, 1970. $8-12

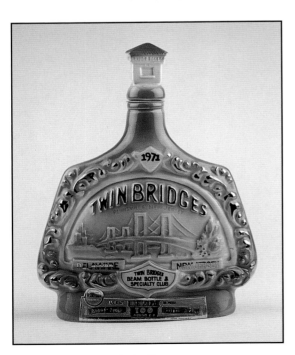

Twin Bridges, 1971. $10-15

California Mission, 1970. "200th Anniversary of California's Missions" on back. $10-15

Fox on a Dolphin, 1980, $20. Red coated fox (not shown), 1973,
$600. Renee the fox, 1974, $15. Runner, 1974, $15. Surfer, 1975,
$15. Uncle Sam fox, 1971, $20.

Left: Milwaukee stein, 1972. $15-20.

Far left: Akron, Rubber Capital of the
World, 1973. Back depicts factory and
worker collecting rubber from tree.
$15-20

Saint Louis Club,
1972. $8-12

Pennsylvania Dutch Club, 1974. $10-15

Wolverine Club, 1964. Story of Michigan wolverine on back. $8-12

Chicago Jim Beam Bottle Club, 1977. "Weekend of fun, frivolity, fellowship" on back. $8-12

Camellia City Club, 1979. "Camellia City Jim Beam Bottle Club #41, Sacramento, Calif." on back. $20-25

Beaver Valley Jim Beam Club, 1977. $8-12

Bean Pot, 1980. "New England Beam and Specialties Club" on back. $10-15

Monterey Club, 1977. $5-10

Republic of Texas Club, 1980. State symbols on back. $10-15

Five Seasons Club, 1980. "The Hawkeye State, Cedar Rapids" on back. $8-12

Gem City Club, 1983. $25-30

Blue Hen Jim Beam and Specialty Club, 1982. $12-18

Convention Series
1971-Present

The first Convention for the National Assocation of Jim Beam Bottle and Specialties Clubs was held in Denver, Colorado in 1971. The Association has met annually since then, in a different location each year. Naturally, each convention features a limited edition bottle to commemorate the event. "His" and "her" convention packages are also available, which include matching "his" and "her" decanters.

Convention bottles were produced by Regal China until 1992; bottles for the 1993 convention and after were produced by Wade Ceramics, Ltd.

For more information about glass convention bottles pictured here, see page 132.

Convention #1, Denver, 1971. Affiliate clubs listed on back. $5-10. There are two versions of the #2 Anaheim decanter. One bears the correct dates of the convention, June 19-25, and values around $20-25. The other has the wrong dates, June 20-23, but the error makes the decanter worth about $50-60.

#3 Detroit, 1973, $10-15. #4 Lancaster, 1974. "Hosted by the Pennsylvania Dutch Club" with other clubs listed on back, $45-50.

#5 Sacramento, 1975, "Camelia City" on back, $5-10. #6 Hartford, Connecticut, 1976, U.S. map on back, $8-12. #7 Louisville, 1977, "My Old Kentucky Home" on back, $8-12.

#8 Chicago, 1978: China ashtray, 1978, $10-15. Giveaway bottle signed by members, $2-5. Decanter, $10-15.

#9 Houston, 1979: Antiqued Houston Cowboy, $25-30. Painted Houston Cowboy, $25-30. Tiffiny on Rocket, $25-30. Giveaway bottles signed by members, $2-5.

#10 Norfolk, 1980: Cup with Renee and the red fox, $5-10. Giveaway bottle, $1-3. Sailing ship, 10th convention, $23-28. Waterman in pewter and yellow, $23-28 each.

#11 Las Vegas, 1981: Showgirls, blonde and brunette, $38-43. Dealer fox, $35-40. Fox and die planter, giveaway bottle, $1-10 each.

#12 New Orleans, 1982: King Rex, $20-25. Buccaneer, color, $20-25. Buccaneer, bronze, $20-25. Ashtray and pitcher, $5-10 each.

#13 St. Louis, 1983: St. Louis Stein, $45-50. Gibson Girl, yellow and blue, $50-55 each. Pitcher, $5-10.

#14 Hollywood, Florida, 1984: Neptune, $20-25. Mermaids, blonde and brunette, $30-35 each. Pitcher and giveaway bottle, $1-10 each.

#15 Las Vegas, 1985: Roulette, $50-55. Fox paperweight, dressed as Caesar, $10-15.

#17 Louisville, 1987: Kentucky Colonels in blue and grey, $55-60 each. Not pictured: Convention bottle, a "framed picture" of a riverboat, similar in design to the Kansas City Covered Wagon decanter, $40-50.

#16, Boston, 1986: Pilgrim Lady, $20-25. Minuteman in Pewter and color, $20-25 each.

#18, 1988: Beaver, $30-35. Portland Rose in red and yellow, $20-25.

#19, Kansas City, 1989: Covered Wagon, $38-42. His (silver) and hers (burgundy) '69 Camaro convertibles were also given away; they are pictured on page 140.

#20, Kissimmee, Florida, 1990: Beach scene bottle, $35-40. Two paperweights, $5-10. His (blue) and hers (cream) '57 Chevy Bel Airs were also given away; they are pictured on page 139.

#21 Reno, 1991: Cowboy fox, $65-70.

#22 St. Louis, 1992: Convention bottle, $45-50. His (green) and Hers (yellow) '68 Corvettes were also available; they are pictured on page 143.

#23 Charlotte, 1993: Convention bottle, $68-73.

#25 Louisville, 1995: Steamboat bottle, $70-75.

#24 Dallas, 1994: Cowboy on Horse, $70-75.
Cowboy boots, silver and gold, $74-75.

#26 Seattle, 1996. $20-25

31

Left: #28, Buffalo, 1998, $55-60. #27, Oconomowoc, Wisconsin, 1997, Deer head, $55-60. Not pictured: Go-withs from both conventions. The Oconomowoc convention offered deer steins in blue, white, and cream, mini steins in blue and cream, and a "Hapy Little Guy" plate in cream. The Buffalo convention offered pitchers in three colors (cream, green, white) featuring James Lockhart's artwork, as well as a green plate.

Above: San Antonio, 1999. Alamo bottle, $75-100. Jugs, $45+. Go-withs, $25 each.

Customer Specialty Series

Angelo's Liquors

1988-1992

Angelo's Liquors commisioned several vehicle decanters to advertise their company. You can find pictures of them with the Wheel Series.

Semi-tractor trailer, 18-wheeler: Angelo's Liquors, bronze & red, 1991, $70-75. Angelo's truck in beige (not shown), $60-65.

- 1964 Gold Mercedes, 1988.
  See page 148

- 1929 Ford Pickup Truck, 1990
  See page 145

- 1957 Corvettes, orange and white, 1990
  See page 143

- Tractor Trailer, bronze and red, 1991
  Pictured below

- '68 Corvettes, red and white, 1992
  See page 143

Harold's Club

1957-1982

Harold's Club bottles include a series that ran parallel to the Executive Series (beginning in 1967), known as the VIP bottles. These are identical to the Executives (see page 50), only they have a "Harold's Club" logo in a prominent place. When looking at bottles with these shapes, be certain to determine whether the bottle is an Executive, Harold's, or Bing Crosby (see page 97); the value of the bottle is directly affected. For instance, the 1969 Harold's bottle is valued at $275, while the 1969 Executive "Sovereign" is valued at only $5-10.

Harold's Silver Opal glass bottle, 1957. $20-25.

Harold's Club: Nevada gray, 1963. "Nevada Centennial 1864-1964" on back, $100. Nevada silver, 1964, $100.

Harold's Club Man in Barrel #1, 1957, $250. Man in Barrel #2, 1958, $150. It's very difficult to find these bottles with the red ties still intact—they were painted, not fired on.

Left: Harold's Club: Pinwheel, 1965. $35-40. Slot Machine, blue, 1967. $10-15. There is also a grey Harold's slot machine that belongs to the Regal China series, pictured on page 79.

Below: Harold's Club: Covered Wagon, 1969. Blue and green. "I Want to Quit Winners" and signature of Harold S. Smith, Sr. on back. $5-10 each.

Harold's Club VIP bottles. 1967, $45-50. 1968, $45-50. 1969, $175.

Harold's Club VIP bottles. 1970, $35-40. 1971, $50-55. 1972, $20-25.

Harold's Club VIP bottles: 1973, $15-20. 1974, $18-22. 1975, $12-17.

Harold's Club VIP bottles: 1976, $20-25. 1977, $22-27. 1978, $22-27.

Harold's Club VIP bottles: 1979, $25-30. 1980, $20-25. 1981, $95-100. 1982, $45-50.

Zimmerman's

1965-1983

Zimmerman's also had a glass bottle; it is pictured on page 121 with the Glass series.

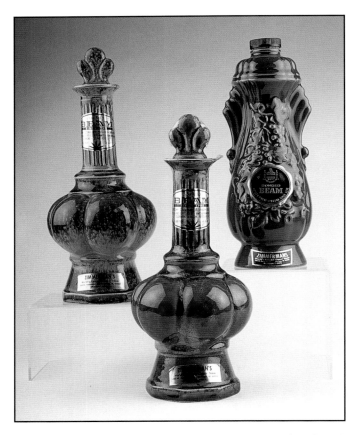

Zimmerman's Liquor Store: Vase, green and brown, $7-12 each. Two-handled jug, 1965, $25-30.

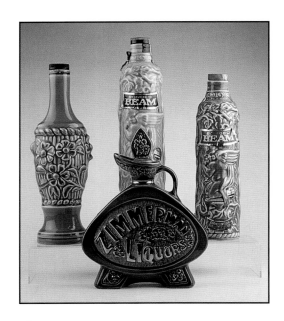

Above: Zimmerman's Liquor Store: Oatmeal China Jug, 1966. $45-50

Left: Zimmerman's Liquor Store. Blue Daisy, 1967, $4-9. Blue Beauty, 1969, with "Zimmerman's Liquors" on back, $10-15. Cherub, 1968, salmon and lavender, $5-10 each.

Zimmerman's Liquor Store: Art Institute, 1972, "Chicago's magnificent mile" on back, $7-12. 50th Anniversary, 1983, "A salute to Zimmerman's" on the back, $30-35.

Zimmerman's Liquor Store: Peddler, 1971, $8-12. Z, 1970, $8-12.

Zimmerman's Bell, light and dark blue, 1976. $8-12

Zimmerman's Liquor Store: El Dorado, marbled green or brown, 1978. $8-12

Other Customer Specialty Bottles
1956-1991

Foremost Liquors Gray and Gold, 1956, $150-160. Foremost Black and Gold, 1956, $130-140.

Pink Speckled Beauty, 1956, $230-240. Only about ten of the mock-up on the right were made, with an experimental glaze that was rejected for not being pink enough. These are worth $300 or more.

The Pheasant Run Resort bottle in the Customer Specialty Series looks identical to this one (which belongs to the trophy series), except the sticker on the base reads "Pheasant Run." These bottles were made from 1960-68. Older bottles are more valuable. $35-40

Harrah's Club, 1963.
Nevada Silver, $500.
Nevada Grey, $350.

Marina City, 1962. $8-12

First National Bank of Chicago, 1964. $1,200.
Paperweight, $30.

Richard's New Mexico, 1967.
State scenes on back. $5-10

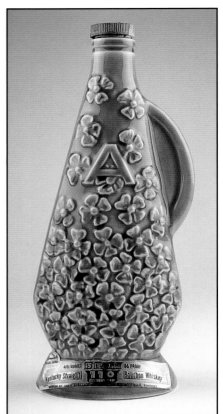

Armanetti "A" Flower Vase. $8-12

Katz. Black, 1968, $10-15. Yellow, 1967, $12-17.

Broadmoor Hotel, 1968. $2-6

Armanetti Liquors, First Award, 1969. "Brand Names Foundation Incorporated Award Winner" and "1968 Retailer of the Year" on back. $8-12

40

Las Vegas Golden Gate Casino, 1969, $60-65. Golden Nugget Casino, 1969, $40-45.

Cal-Neva, 1968. "Reno: The biggest little city in the world" on back. $5-8

Harry Hoffman liquor store, 1969. Skier on the back. $5-10

Harvey Hotel, 1969, $10-15.
Herre Brothers, 1972, $25-30.

41

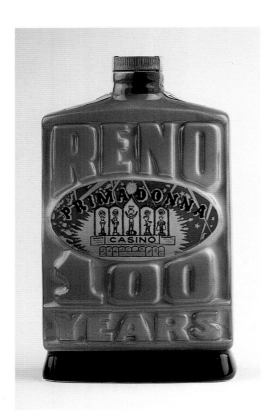

Prima Donna Casino, 1969. $7-12

Horseshoe Club, Reno, Nevada, 1969. $8-12

Binions Horseshoe Hotel Casino, 1970. "See $1,000,000 in cash" on back. $8-12

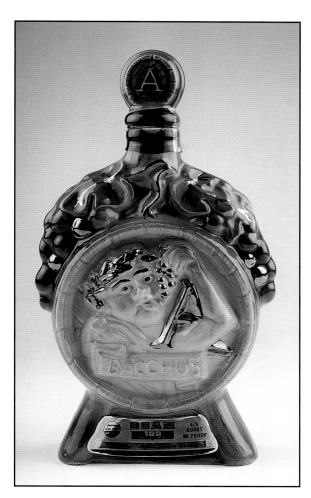

Golden Gate Casino, 1969, $75. 1970 (pictured), $10-15.

Bacchus, 1970. "Armanetti, Serving Chicago since 1933 with pleasure" on back. $8-12

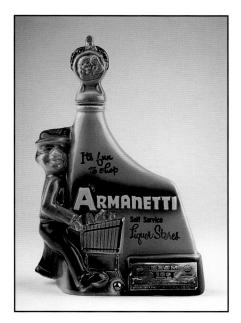

Armanetti Shopper, "It's Fun to Shop," 1971. State of Illinois on back. $8-12

Hyatt House, Chicago, 1971, $8-12. Hyatt Regency, New Orleans, 1976, $9-13.

Smith's North Shore Club, 1972. "Lake Tahoe, Crystal Bay" on back. $10-15

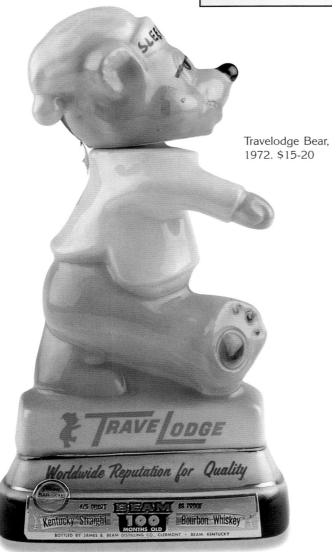

Travelodge Bear, 1972. $15-20

Cherry Hills Country Club, 1973. "Golden Anniversary, 1922-1972, USGA Open" on back. $15-25

Ponderosa Ranch, 1972. "One millionth tourist" on back. $13-18

Hawaiian Open: Golfball, 1973, $20-25.

Ralph's Market, 1973. $10-15

ABC Lounges, Florida, 1973. Back depicts palm trees and "ABC" sign. $10-15

Bohemian Girl, 1974. "Bohemian Cafe, Omaha, Nebraska" on back. $15-20

Sheraton Hotel, 1974. $5-10

Ramada Inn, 1976. "Ramada Tradition" on back. $2-7

Ernie's Flower Cart, 1976. "San Francisco" on back. $25-30

Spenger's Fish Grotto, 1977. "14th Street, Berkeley, California" on back. $15-20

Above: Nutcracker, 1978, $75-80. Matching paperweight, $25.

Left: GM Parts Division, Mr. Goodwrench, 1979. $40-45

Von's Market, 1981.
$25-30

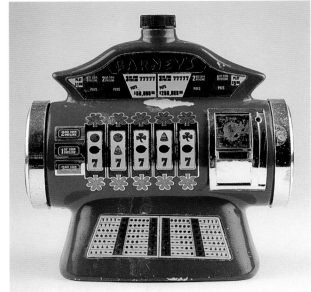

Barney's Slot Machine, 1978. $25-30

Jewel T Man, 1982.
$65-70

Circus Circus clown, 1987. $45-50

Harley-Davidson Decanter, 85th anniversary, 1988. Limited edition #110 out of 3,000. 1987. Very difficult to find. $250+. Not Pictured: Harley-Davidson Stein, also rare, 1988. $200+.

Osco Drugs, 1987. $18-22

Semi-tractor trailer, 18-wheeler, Food for Less. $400

Executive Series

1955-1987

The first bottle in this series (1955, Royal Porcelain) is one of the first decorative ceramic decanters offered by Jim Beam. Executive bottles were released yearly around the Christmas holidays from 1955 through 1987. These are some of the most beautifully ornate bottles produced; some of them include decoration in 22-carat gold.

Beginning with 1967, very similar bottles, differing only in color, were issued with Beam Company presidents' signatures for the Presidential series; several are pictured here. *For more information about the Presidential Series, please see page 77.*

Black Royal Porcelain, 1955, $150. Royal Gold Round, 1956, $100-110. Royal Di Monte, 1957, $65-70. Grey Cherub, 1958, $85-95. Tavern Scene, 1959, $35-40.

Blue Cherub, 1960, $45-50. Golden Chalice, 1961, $22-27. Flower Basket, 1962, $25-30. Royal Rosé, 1963, $18-23. Royal Gold Diamond, 1964, $22-27.

Marbled Fantasy, 1965, $25-30. Majestic, 1966, $12-17. Prestige, 1967, $10-15. Presidential, 1968, $10-15. Sovereign, 1969, $5-10.

Charisma, 1970, $12-17. Fantasia, 1971, $12-17. Regency, 1972, $10-15. Phoenician, 1973, $10-15. Twin Cherubs, 1974, $10-15.

Reflections, 1975, $10-15. Floro De Oro, 1976, $12-17. Golden Jubilee, 1977, $12-17. Texas Rose (Regal China series), 1978, $13-18. Yellow Rose, 1978, $13-18.

Mother of Pearl, 1979, $15-20. The same bottle, in green, signed by Beam president J.J. McShane, $50-55.

Antique Pitcher, 1982, $18-23. Green bottle signed by J.J. McShane, $45-50. (Pitchers were made for the twelve districts that make up the International Jim Beam Club. Colors were as follows: District #1 rose; 2 green; 3 rust; 4 light blue; 5 brown; 6 dark blue; 7 peach; 8 mustard; 9 beige; 10 light blue; 11 speckled grey; 12 grey.)

Titian, 1980, $12-17. There is an identical bottle, signed by McShane (not pictured) worth $65-70. Titian in blue, signed by J.J. McShane, $80-85. Royal Filigree "Cobalt" Deluxe, 1981, $5-10. Identical bottle, signed by McShane (not pictured) worth $50-55. Royal Filigree in green, signed by J.J. McShane, $80-85.

Bell music box, with partridge, 1983, $33-38. Signed by J.J. McShane, $45-50. Bell music box, with carollers, 1984, $20-25. Same bell, signed by Beam president Barry M. Berish, $95-100. (Bells with partridge were made for the twelve districts that make up the International Jim Beam Club. Colors were as follows: District #1 tan; 2 light blue; 3 green; 4 oatmeal; 5 peach; 6 dark brown; 7 slate blue; 8 unknown; 9 dark blue; 10 unknown; 11 tan; 12 unknown. Bells with carollers were also made for the twelve districts. Colors were as follows: District #1 ivory; 2 grey; 3 tan; 4 green; 5 oatmeal; 6 peach; 7 tan; 8 light blue; 9 dark brown; 10 dark blue; 11 slate blue; 12 rust.)

Twin doves, 1987, in white, $15-20. In yellow, signed by Barry Berish, $45-50.

Italian marble urns in several colors (not shown), worth $18-23. Urn signed by Barry Berish, 1985, $45-50. District urn, $28-33. Blue Font, 1986, $25-30.

Famous People
1970-1985

Paul Bunyan, 1970. $8-12

Buffalo Bill, 1971. $15-20

General John Stark, 1972.
"Bennington Battle Flag, August 16,
1777" on back. $13-18

Right: John Henry, 1972. "The Legend of John Henry" on the back. $30-35

Far right: King Kamehameha, 1972. $15-20

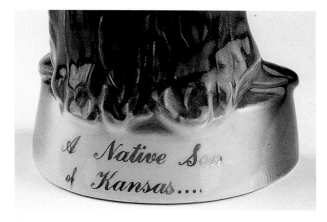

Close-up of Kansas signature on Emmett Kelly bottle.

Emmett Kelly, 1973. Unsigned, $30-35. Signed with Kansas autograph, $70-75.

Hatfield, 1973, and McCoy, 1973. $18-23 each

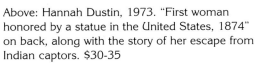

Above: Hannah Dustin, 1973. "First woman honored by a statue in the United States, 1874" on back, along with the story of her escape from Indian captors. $30-35

Right: Rocky Marciano, 1973. "Rocky's Record of Achievement" listed on back. $40-45

George Washington and Martha Washington, 1976. Biographies on back. $15-25

Hank Williams, Jr., 1985. "A golden salute to one of country music's best-loved performers" on back. $30-35

American cowboy, 1981. Regular, $18-22. Pewter, $150.

Foreign Country Series
1969-1985

Fiji Island, 1971. "Cession 1874, 1970 Independence" on back. $8-12.

Germany, Weisbaden, 1973, dancers and grapes on back, $5-10. Germany, Pied Piper, 1974, "World Soccer Championship, Munich 1974" on back, $20-25.

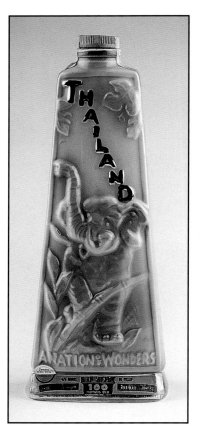

Above: Thailand, 1969. Dancer and country map on back. $4-9

Left: Koala Bear, Australia, 1973. There are both grey and brown bears, the brown worth about twice as much as the grey. $15-35

Samoa, 1973. $8-12

Australian Tigers rugby team, 1977. $20-25

Kiwi bird, New Zealand, 1974,
$10-15. Magpies rugby team,
Australia, 1977, $10-15.

Kangaroo, Australia, 1977. $15-20

Sydney Opera House, 1977. $20-25

Queensland, Australia, 1978. Star with state animals on back. $20-25

Gallah Bird, Australia, 1980. $20-25

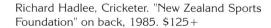

Swagman, 1979. "2nd National Convention, Australian Beam Bottle Clubs, 1979" on back. $20-25

Owl—LVNH (Licensed Victuallers National Homes), 1982. This group was founded in 1824 to provide retirement housing for public house licensees. The owl represents British pub licensees association. $15-20

Richard Hadlee, Cricketer. "New Zealand Sports Foundation" on back, 1985. $125+

Holiday Series
1983-1991

Similar bottles were produced in different colors for the Presidential Series. *For more information about the Presidential Series, please see page 77.*

Holiday Carollers, 1988, (not pictured) $50-55. The Holiday Carollers is identical to the Presidential bottle pictured here, except it is colorfully painted. Carollers, signed by Barry Berrish (Presidential), $45-50.

Christmas nutcracker series: 1989 Holiday Nutcracker, $45-50. Plain brown signed by Barry Berrish (Presidential series), $45-50. 1990 Nutcracker drum, $18-23. Silver signed by Barry Berrish (Pesidential series), $65-75. 1991 Holiday Nutcracker, $33-38. Gold, signed by Barry Berrish (Presidential series), $30-35.

One-of-a-Kind Bottles
1975-Present

One-of-a-kind bottles began in 1975 as a charity fundraiser for Beam clubs. A one-of-a-kind bottle was raffled off, and proceeds from ticket sales benefitted the clubs, the International Association, and the Boy's Town of Italy Scholarship Fund. The drive received a tremendous response from Beamers across the nation, earning over $20,000 and a guarantee that the one-of-a-kind contest would continue for years to come.

The one-of-a-kind bottles are, to say the least, difficult to come by—but they are out there. The first, offered in the 1975 contest, featured caricatures of IAJBB&SC past presidents Jerry Wingenroth, Louis Iannarone, and Paul Saroff standing in a circle with a globe resting on their backs. Other bottles incorporated similar presidential caricatures, designs from convention bottles, Rennie the fox, even images of the First National Bank bottle and the Agnew elephant.

Opera Series
1977-1982

The Opera Series decanters are valuable and difficult to come by. The pieces all came with their own stands, and are music boxes. Most of them also have matching paperweights.

Nutcracker, 1978, $75-80; matching paperweight, $25.

New Zealand Opera characters: Hongi Hika, 1980, $140. Hone Heke, 1981, $155. Terauparaha, 1982, $155.

Aida, 1978, $90-95; matching paperweight (not shown), $25. Falstaff, 1979, $125-130; Madam Butterfly, 1976, $195-225; matching paperweight, $50.

Carmen, 1978, $75-95; matching paper-
weight, $25. Figaro, 1977, $75-95; matching
paperweight, $25. Mephistopheles, 1979,
$170-175; matching paperweight, $35.

Don Giovanni, 1980, $95-110; matching paperweight, $35. Boris
Godunov, 1982, $150-175; matching paperweight, $35.

Organization Series
1968-1986

Yuma Club, 1968. "Arizona" on back. $15-20

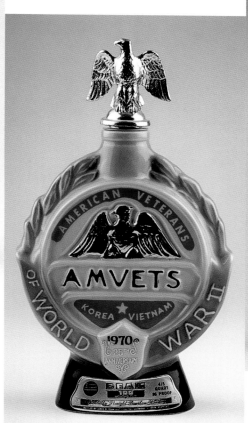

Kentucky Colonels, 1970. $10-15

Amvets, 1970. "25th Anniversary" on back. $5-10

Left: Shriners. Indiana, 1970, state outline on back, $3-8. Moila with camel, 1974, sword and crescent moon on back, $20-25. Moila with sword, 1972, Mecca and pilgrims on back, $20-25.

Above: Shriners. Pyramid-Cedar Rapids El Kahir Temple, 1975, $12-17. Rajah pretzel, 1977, "Home of the Pretzel Bowl since 1951, Reading, PA" on back, $22-27. Western Shrine Association, 1980, "Shrinedom Aglow in Eight-O" on back, $15-20.

Order of the Blue Goose Int., 1971. "Green Lakes, Wisc., 1906" on back. $5-10

BPO Does, 1971. "Benevolent patriotic Order of Does" on back. $5-10

Elks, 1968, "1868-1969" on stopper back, $2-7. Elks National Foundation, 1977, short history and "1928-1978" on back, $8-12.

Pearl Harbor Survivors Association, 1976, "U.S.S. *Arizona* Memorial" on back, $15-20. Pearl Harbor, 1976, "Oahu" on back, $10-15.

V.F.W., 1971. "50th Anniversary, Department of Indian V.F.W." on back. $4-9

Ahepa, 1972. Back of the bottle has picture of open book with membership list of "Mother Lodge" and "Supreme Lodge." $5-10

Bartenders' Guild, 1973. $5-10

Phi Sigma Kappa, 1973. $25-30

CRLDA, 1973. "California Retail Liquor Dealers Association" on back. $8-12

CPO Mess, 1974. "Grand Opening,
Navy's No. 1 Club." $8-12

Fleet Reserve, 1974. "50 Years of Service ...
The Fleet Reserve Association celebrates its
first half century, Philadelphia, PA" on back.
$2-5

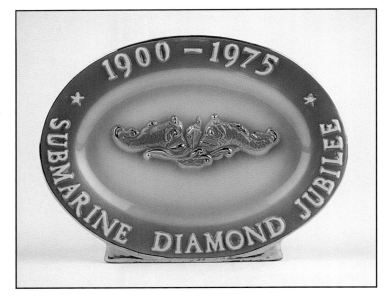

Submarine Diamond Jubilee, 1977. "U.S. Submarine Veterans,
World War II" on back. $20-25

Bowling Proprietors, 1974. Casino picture and "Sahara,
Lake Tahoe, Nevada" on back. $8-12

National Licensed Beverage Association, 1974. "25th Anniversary" on back. $5-10

Turtle Long Neck, 1975. "How Sweet it Is" on back, $16-21. Turtle Short Neck, 1975, $10-15.

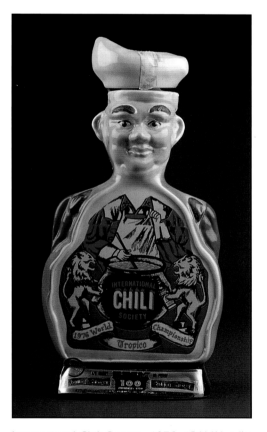

International Chili Society, 1976. "C.V. Wood's World Championship Chili" recipe on back. $10-15.

Sports Car Club of America, 1976. History of club on back. Smooth, $12-17. Etched, $18-23.

Sturgeon, 1980. $45-50

Sigma Nu Fraternity. Kentucky, 1977, $15-20. Michigan, 1977, $18-22.

Homebuilders Association, 1979. "Home Builders Convention, Las Vegas" on back. $20-25

Legion Music, 1978. "National Contest Championships" listed on back. $8-12

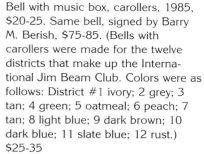

Bell with music box, carollers, 1985, $20-25. Same bell, signed by Barry M. Berish, $75-85. (Bells with carollers were made for the twelve districts that make up the International Jim Beam Club. Colors were as follows: District #1 ivory; 2 grey; 3 tan; 4 green; 5 oatmeal; 6 peach; 7 tan; 8 light blue; 9 dark brown; 10 dark blue; 11 slate blue; 12 rust.) $25-35

Christmas Santa, 1983, $100-110; matching paperweight, $20-25. One-of-a-kind Santa, signed by the artist and J.J. McShane, 1983.

District urn, $28-33.

Snowman, 1984, $130-135; matching paperweight, $25-30. Noel candle, 1987, $145-150; matching paperweight, $25-30. Christmas Tree, 1986, $100-110; matching paperweight, $25-30.

Oregon Liquor Control Commission. "OLCC, 1934-1984" on back. $30-35

Ducks Unlimited
1974-1995

Some of the most beautiful Beam bottles around were produced for the Ducks Unlimited society. The organization commisioned a new bottle each year. The decanters were sold in liquor stores with a portion of the proceeds donated to Ducks Unlimited.

A Ducks Unlimited clock was also produced for the Regal China series (see page 93).

Not pictured here is the 1993 Ducks Unlimited bottle, which features the Cinnamon Teal, as well as the 1984 Mallard bottle.

Ducks Unlimited bottles. Mallard, 1974, $20-25. Wood Duck, 1975, $20-25. Mallard Hen, 1977, $30-35. Mallard Head, 1978, $30-35.

Ducks Unlimited bottles. Canvasback Drake, 1979, $43-48. Blue Winged Teal pair, 1980, $27-31. Green Winged Teal pair, 1981, $36-41. Wood Duck Family, 1982, $63-68.

American Widgeon Pair, 1983, $62-67. Mallard, special edition for the Peabody Hotel, very rare, $150. Pintail pair, 1985, $35. Mallard 1988 Duck Decoy. Member of the Trophy Series, $40-45. Not shown: 1984 Ducks Unlimited Mallard pair, $80-85.

Redhead, 1986, $40-50. Bluebill, 1987, $30-35. Gadwalls, 1986, $45-50. Black Ducks, 1989, $93-98.

Canada Goose, 1990, $53-58.
Ringneck, 1992, $77-82.
Tundra Swan, 1991, $35-40.

Loon, 1992, $300. This bottle, which is very rare, was not approved by Ducks Unlimited, so the Ringneck was offered in its place as the 1992 bottle.

Harlequin Duck, 1994, $95-100. The only duck in the series with a miniature, $40-45. Not pictured: 1993 Cinnamon Teal, $100-125. Both the Harlequin and Cinnamon Teal decanters were made by Ski Country for the Jim Beam Association after Regal China closed.

73

Political Series
1956-1988

These bottles were released for election years.

Ashtray, donkey and elephant, 1956. $15-20 each

Agnew Elephant, 1970. About 65 were made and distributed at a fundraiser for Spiro Agnew's vice-presidential campaign. The bottle is very fragile. $750

Campaigner, donkey and elephant, 1960. $15-20 each

Boxer, donkey and elephant, 1964. Scotch and bourbon bottles have different labels and hat-bands. $15-20 each

Clown, donkey and elephant, 1968.
$10-15 each

Miami Beach elephant, 1972. Nomination for the re-election of Richard Nixon, $240.
With plate, $350.

Football, elephant and donkey, 1972, $15-20. San Diego
Elephant, 1972, $15-20.

Washington DC Elephant, 1972. Given out to the executive
committee at a Republican dinner. $300

Superman, donkey and elephant, 1980. $18-22 each

Drum, donkey and elephant, 1976, $8-12 each. Kansas City Convention elephant, 1976, $22-27. New York Convention donkey, 1976, $18-22.

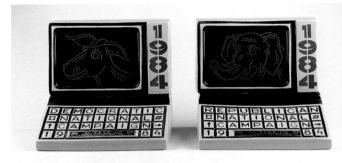

Computer, donkey and elephant, 1984. $28-32 each

Drummer, donkey and elephant, 1988. $35-40 each

Presidential Series

1979-1991

The presidential series consists of an assortment of bottles given yearly by the James B. Beam Distilling Company as Christmas presents to each club belonging to the International Association. These bottles are similar in shape to certain Executive and Holiday bottles, but are in different colors and signed by the company's presidents.

- Julian McShane, 1979 *See page 52*
- Julian McShane, 1980 *See page 52*
- Julian McShane, 1981 *See page 52*
- Julian McShane, 1982 *See page 52*
- Julian McShane, 1983 *See page 53*
- Barry Berish, 1984 *See page 53*
- Barry Berish, 1985 *See page 53*
- Barry Berish, 1986 *See page 53*
- Barry Berish, 1987 *See page 53*
- Barry Berish, 1988 *See right*
- Barry Berish, 1989 *See page 62*
- Barry Berish, 1990 *See page 62*
- Barry Berish, 1991 *See page 62*

Holiday Carollers, signed by Barry Berrish (Presidential), 1988, $45-50.

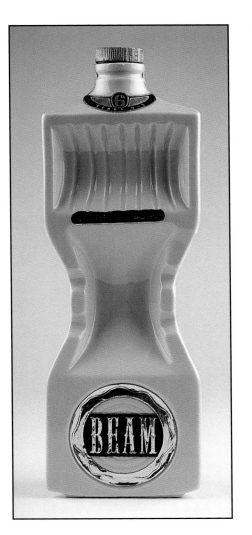

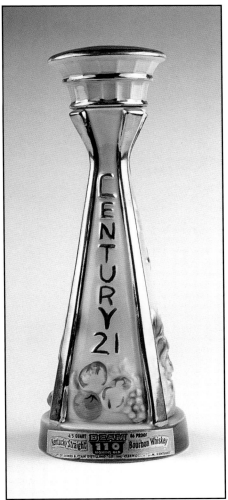

Regal China

1955-1992

Far left: Beam ashtray, white, 1955. This was the first ceramic design for decorative Beam decanters. $12-18

Left: Space Needle, Seattle World's Fair, 1962. $15-20

Musicians on a Wine Cask, 1964.
$5-10

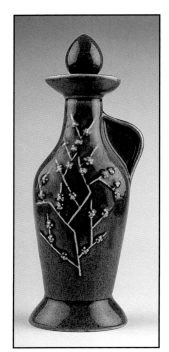

Green China Jug, aka "the
Pussy Willow", 1965. $5-10

New York World's Fair, 1964. $12-17

Redwood Empire, 1967. Map of
California's Pacific Coast on
back. $4-9.

Turquoise China Jug,
1964. $2-7

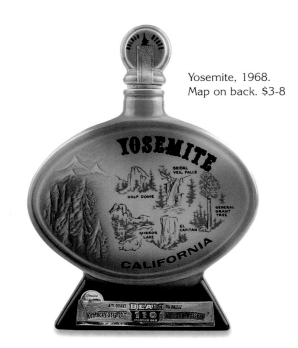

Yosemite, 1968.
Map on back. $3-8

Slot Machine, grey, 1968. A nearly identical decanter was issued in blue for the Customer Specialty series. $8-12

Hemisfair, Texas, 1968. Scenic Texas pictures on back. $8-12

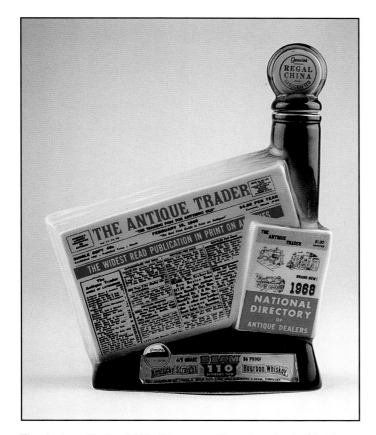

The Antique Trader, 1968. "Kewanee, Illinois" on back. $5-10

Pony Express, 1968. Map on back. $5-10.

Cable Car, 1968, $5-10

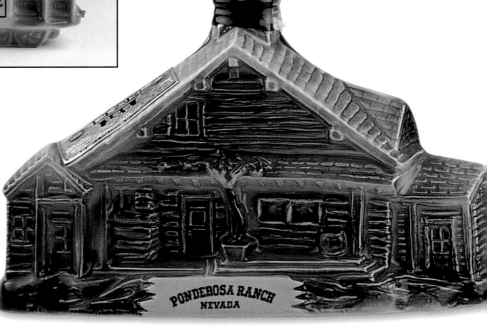

Ponderosa Ranch House, 1969.
"Lake Tahoe" on back. $12-17

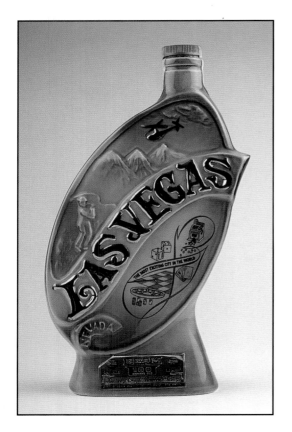

Far left: Las Vegas, 1969.
Hoover Dam on back. $8-12

Left: Bell Scotch, 1969. "Bell's
Royal Vat" on back. $5-10

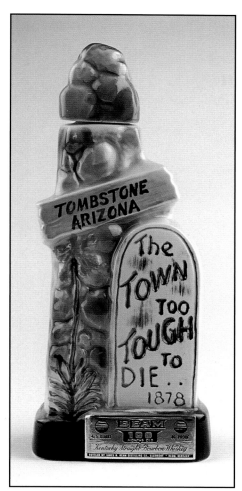

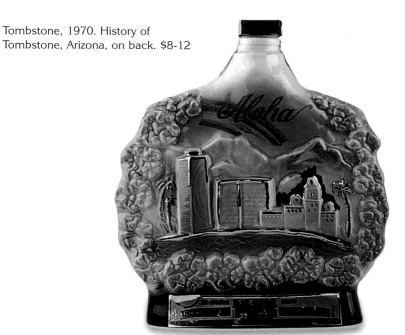

Tombstone, 1970. History of Tombstone, Arizona, on back. $8-12

Hawaii "Aloha" with King Kamehameha, 1971. $15-20

Franklin Mint, 1970. Liberty Bell on back. $5-10

Bell Ringer—"Afore Ye Go", 1970. Bell Ringer Plaid, 1970. $5-10 each

New Hampshire with golden eagle, 1971. History of the wooden eagle carving on the State House on back. $20-25

London Bridge, 1971. $5-10. With medallion, shown on back along with history of the bridge, $45-50.

Tall Cedars of Lebanon. "National Charitable Objective...Labor Day New York City Telethon, 1971" on back. $5-10

Petroleum Man, International Petroleum Exposition, 1971. "Tulsa: Oil Capital of the World" on back. $5-10

Permian Basin Oil Show, 1972. $5-10

The Great Chicago Fire, 1971. Brief history on back. $18-23

Portland Rose Festival, 1972. "For You a Rose in Portland Grows" with history of the festival on back. $8-12

Tobacco Festival, 1973. "Richmond, VA 1973." $15-20.

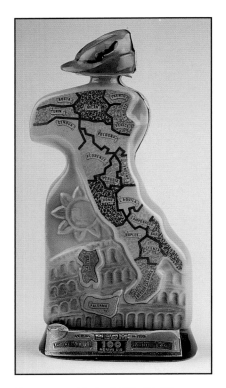

Boystown of Italy, 1973. $5-10

Ohio State Fair, 1973. "The 120ᵗʰ Ohio State Fair" on back. $5-10

Viking, 1973. $20-25

World's Fair, 1974. $5-10

Stone Mountain, Georgia, 1974. Story of confederate shrine and other points of interest on back. $18-22

Truth or Consequences Fiesta, 1974. History of town name on back. $2-7

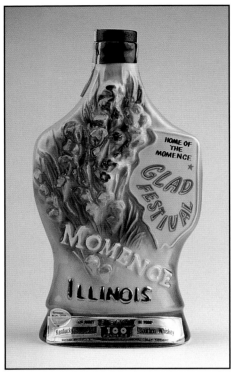

Gladiolas Festival, 1974. "Nation's Oldest Drum & Bugle Competition" on back. $5-10

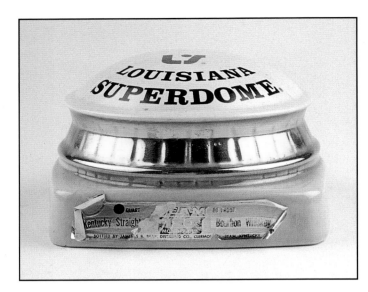

New Orleans Superdome, 1970. $15-20

Bonded, gold and silver, 1975. $5-10

King Kong, 1976. Announcement commemorating movie release on back. $20-25

Charlie McCarthy, 1976. $40-45

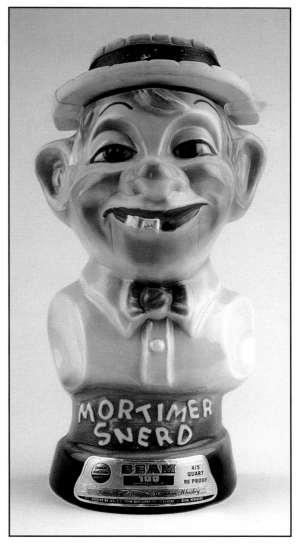

Mortimer Snerd, 1976. $40-45

Texas Rose, 1978. $13-18

AC Spark Plug, 1977. $32-37

Delco Battery, 1978. $22-27

Dark Eyes Vodka Jug, 1978.
Brown and oatmeal. $5-10

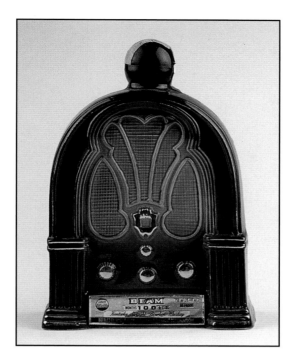

Left: Radio, 1979. Names of Pacific Pioneer Broadcasters founders, directors, and presidents on back. $14-19

Below: Coffee Mill, 1980. $12-18

New York, The Big Apple, 1979. $25-30

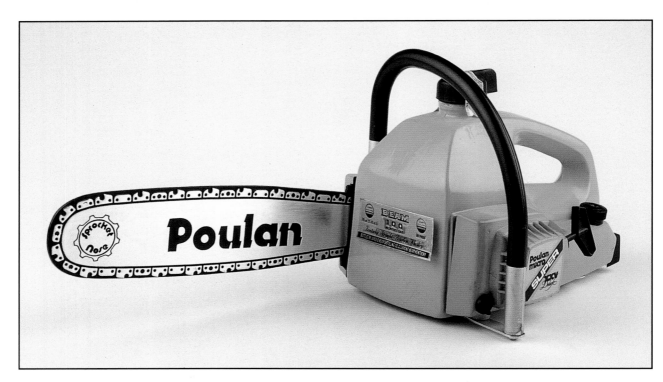

Poulan Chain Saw, 1979. A favorite among outdoorsmen. $30-40

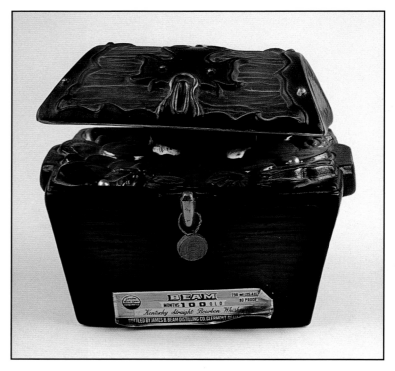

Bonded-Mystic. $6-8

Light bulb with Thomas Edison, 1979. History of Edison's legacy on back. $15-20

Treasure Chest, 1980. $8-12

Indian Chief, 1980. $18-22

Captain and Mate, 1980. $20-22

Antique Globe, 1980. $10-15

Antique Clock, 1985. $30-35

Jim Beam Jug, 1982. $20-25

Stein, German, 1983. $10-15

Mount St. Helens, 1980. "An awesome natural phenomenon" and story, along with a small tube of ash from the explosion. $20-25

Space Shuttle, 1986. $50-55

Ducks Unlimited Clock, 1985. $75-100

Seoul, 1988. $18-22

Fireman Helmet, 1990. Black, $52-57; White, $50-55.

Leprechaun, 1991. $20-25

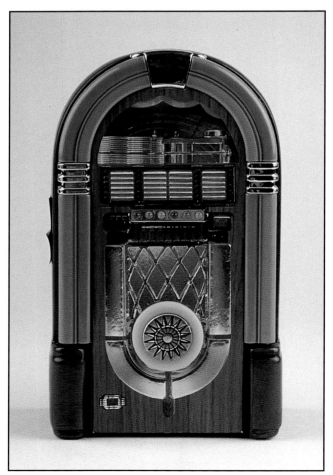

Jukebox, 1990. $60-65

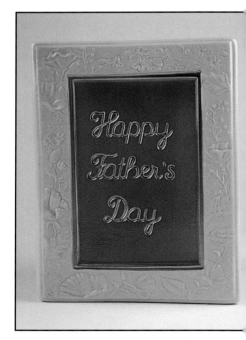

Happy Father's Day, 1998. "Here's to the man..." on back, with "to and from" tag. $18-22

Regal Special Series

1982-1992

The Regal Special Series consists of five jugs, thirteen vehicles, and one Ducks Unlimited decanter, all listed below. Some of these cars and trucks were produced in very limited numbers. Some of the Regal Special vehicle decanters are pictured with the Wheel Series, as noted in the listing. The ones that are not pictured have "cousins" in the Wheel Series that vary only in color.

- German Jug, 1982.
- Beam Jugs, in green, light blue, dark blue, and black, 1982. *Pictured below.*
- Police car, yellow, 1983
- '34 Police car, yellow, 1989. Produced in a limited edition of 700, available to club members attending the 1989 Convention in Kansas City. *See photo on page 150*
- '69 Camaro, green, 1989. Produced in a limited edition of 600.
- '57 Corvette, arctic blue, 1990. *See photo on page 143*
- '63 Corvette, green, 1991.
- '70 Dodge Challenger, blue, 1991. Produced in a limited edition of 800. *See photo on page 157*
- '59 Cadillac, white, limited edition, 1991. *See photo on page 144*
- Tractor trailer, gold, 1991. Produced in a limited edition of 10.
- '59 Cadillac, mint green, 1992. Produced in a limited edition of 500. *See photo on page 144*
- '68 Corvette, bronze, 1992. Produced in a limited edition of 100.
- '68 Corvette, silverstone, 1992. Produced in a limited edition of 12.
- '57 Chevy Bel Air, white, limited edition, 1992.
- '70 Dodge Challenger, green, limited edition, 1992. *See photo on page 157*
- Ducks Unlimited Loon, 1992. *Pictured below.*

Loon, 1992, $300.

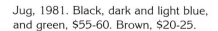

Jug, 1981. Black, dark and light blue, and green, $55-60. Brown, $20-25.

Sports

1968-1991

Sports bottles have remained popular over the years and often command higher prices in the market than bottles from other series.

Football

1972-1989

One member of this series that is not pictured here is a 1989 football decanter that values at about $50-60.

Bob Devaney, Nebraska football coach, 1972. $20-30

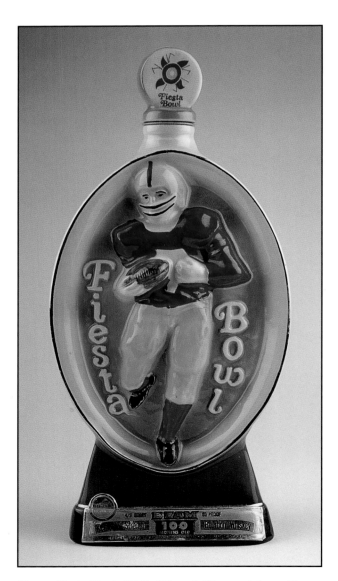

Football Hall of Fame, 1972. Information on the museum written on back. $20-25

Above: Fiesta Bowl, 1973. "Phoenix*Tempe Arizona Dec. 23" on back. $15-20

Right: Hula Bowl, 1974. $25-30. Prototype, which leans slightly farther back, shown on the right. $50 or more.

Golf

1970-1991

Missing from this section is the 1991 Pebble Beach AT&T Golf Tournament decanter, which values around $150-165.

Bing Crosby

Bing Crosby 32nd, 1973, $30-40. Bing Crosby 33rd, 1973, $30-40. Bing Crosby 34th, 1974, $60-70.

Bing Crosby 30th, 1971, $20-30. Bing Crosby National Pro-Am, 29th, 1970, $15-20. Bing Crosby 31st, 1972, $35-45.

Bing Crosby 35th, 1975, $40-50. Bing Crosby 36th, 1976, $35-45. Bing Crosby 37th, 1977, $35-45.

Hawaiian Open

Hawaiian Open. Menehune with two different cloth outfits, 1974, $25-30 each. Disk, 1975, $20-25. Outrigger, 1975, $25-30.

Hawaiian Open. Pineapple, 1972, $20-25. Golf Ball, 1973, $20-25. The Golf Ball decanter actually belongs to the Customer Specialty series. Tiki God, 1974, $20-25.

Left: Bob Hope 14th, 1973, Country club names on back, $45-50. Bob Hope Desert Classic, 1974, "Participating country clubs" on back, $45-50.

Above: Professional Golfer's Association, 1971. Map of PGA National Golf Club, East Course, on back. $20-25

WGA, 1971. "Golf's favorite charity" on back. $15-20

Sahara Invitational, 1971. "$150,000" with names of past winners on back. $15-20

Kaiser International, 1971. "Kaiser International Open" on back. $20-25

US Open, 1972. $45-50

Glen Campbell, 1976. "51st Lost Angeles Open, Riviera Country Club" on back. $22-27

Horse Racing
1968-1978

Churchill Downs, Kentucky Derby, winners shown on the backs. 95th running with Red Roses, 1969, $20-25. 95th with Pink Roses, 1969, $25-30. 96th running, 1970, $25-30. 96th running, with roses on both sides of stopper, $75-100.

Ruidoso Downs, 1968. With pointed ears, $65-75. With ears down, $15-20. Notice the horse-head tops are interchangeable with the horse-head stoppers on the Kentucky bottles in the State series.

Churchill Downs, Kentucky Derby. 97th running, 1971, $20-25. 98th running, 1972, $30-35. 100th running, 1974, $20-25.

Preakness 100th Race, 1975, "This souvenir bottle commemorates..." on back, $20-25. Preakness, 100th Anniversary, 1970, "95th Preakness" on back, $20-25.

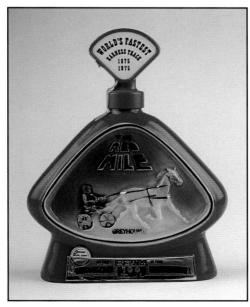

The Red Mile, 1975. Story of the harness track on back. $10-15

Louisville Downs, 1978. Signed statement by William H. King on back. $15-20

Auto Racing
1970-1976

Mint 400, 3rd, 1970. "Del Webb's ... world's greatest off road event" on back. With china stopper, $100. With metal stopper, $10-15. Mint 400, 4th, 1971, "Del Webb Desert Rally" on back, $10-15.

Indianapolis Speed Race, 1970. "The world's greatest sports spectacle: 1911-1970" on back. $12-17

Mint 400. 5th, 1972, statement by management and staff on back, $10-15. 6th, 1973, embossed dune buggy on back, $10-15. 7th, 1975, motorcycle and dune buggy on golden back, $10-12. 8th, 1976, black and white race scene on back, $15-20.

Other Sports
1969-1985

Seattle Seafair, 1960. Boating scene on back. $15-20

Clint Eastwood Invitational Celebrity Tennis Tournament, 1973. "Pebble Beach, July, 1973" on back. $25-30

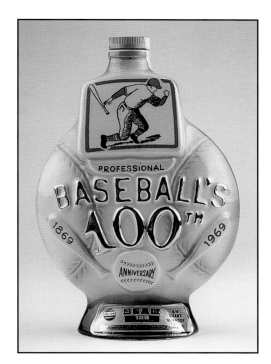

Baseball, 1969. "Professional Baseball's First 100 years" on back, with history. $35-60

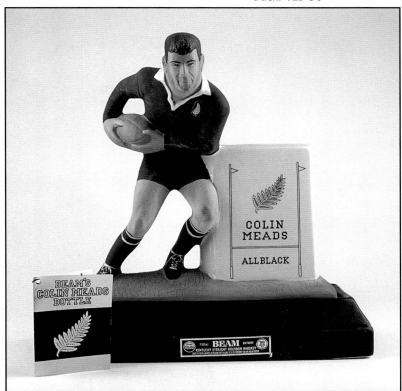

Colin Meads, 1984. "New Zealand Sports Foundation" on back. $150+

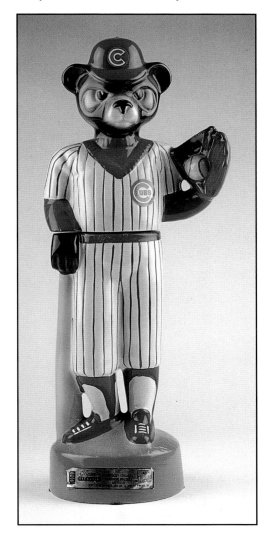

Chicago cubs, 1985. $100-125

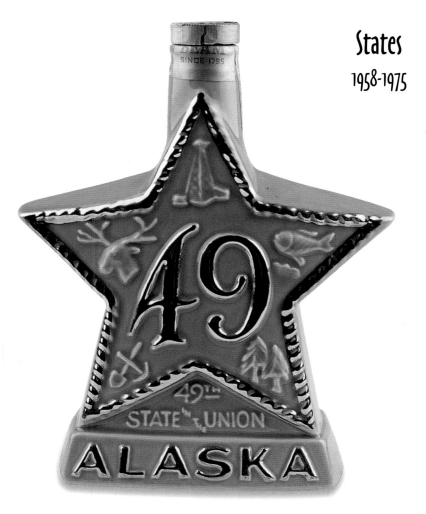

Alaska Star, 1958. Same bottle made for 1964 and 1965. Rope-trimmed star on back. Hard to find. $30-35

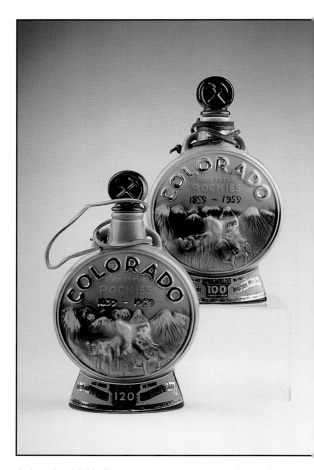

Colorado, 1959. Bottles shown in two shades with different labels. "Colorado Rush to the Rockies Centennial" on back. $25-30

Hawaii, 1959. Shown front and back. $35-40

Oregon, 1959. "Oregon Centennial" on back. $20-25

Kansas, 1960. $40-45

Idaho, 1962, $30-35. Illinois, 1968, $5-10. An embossed stopper (not pictured) on the Illinois bottle adds approximately $5 in value.

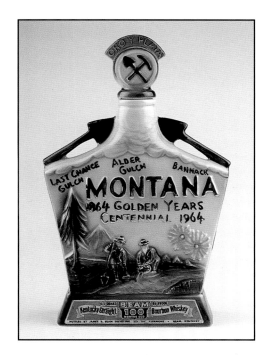

Montana, 1963. Covered wagon on back. $65-70

West Virginia, 1963. "Blackwater Falls" scene on back. $120

New Jersey, 1963. Blue and yellow, with scotch and bourbon in each. $35-40 each

Nebraska, 1967, covered wagon on back, $5-10. Nevada, 1963, silver letters, man with mule on back, $25-30. Nevada, 1964, gold letters (not pictured), $100.

North Dakota, 1964. $35-40

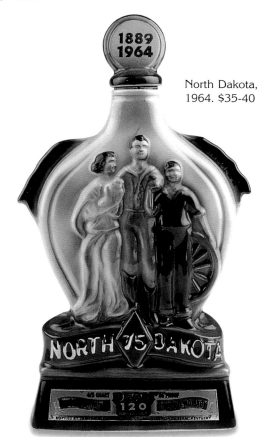

Wyoming, 1965. Old Faithful on back. $45-50

Ohio, 1966. $5-10

Kentucky, 1967. Black head horse, $10-15. Brown head horse, $22-27. White head horse, $22-27. Stoppers are interchangeable with the Ruidoso Downs horse-head stoppers, found in the Sports series.

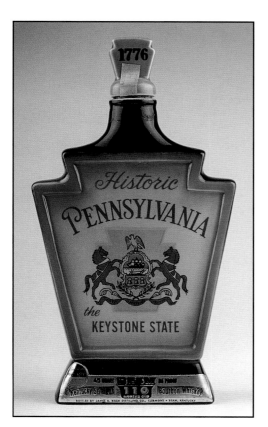

Pennsylvania, 1967. State scenes on back. $10-15

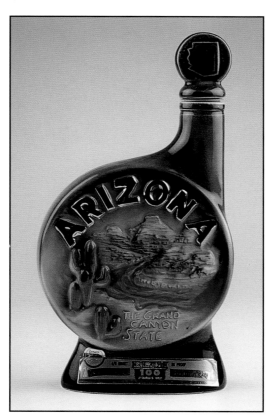

Arizona, 1968. Scenic spots pictured on back. $5-10

New Hampshire, 1967. Map with attractions on back. $5-10

Florida Shell, bronze and pearl. Weinkle Liquor Store labels adds $2-5 in value. $3-8

Maine, 1970. "150th Anniversary" on back. $5-10

Above: South Dakota, Mt. Rushmore, 1969. Info about memorial on back. $8-12

Right: South Carolina, 1970. $5-10

Blue Hen State, Delaware, 1972. $7-10

Michigan, 1972. Thumbnail description of the state's topography and industry on back. $5-10

Washington State, Apple, 1975. $12-17

New Mexico Wedding Vase, 1972. State symbols on back. $12-17

Telephones
1975-1983

Telephone Pioneers of America: Telephone #1, 1907 Wall, 1975, $20-25. Telephone #2, Candlestick, 1978, $25-30. Telephone #3, 1928 French Cradle, 1979, $20-25.

Telephone #4, 1919 Dial, 1980, $45-50. Telephone #5, Pay, 1981, $45-50.

Telephone #6, Battery, 1982, $40-45. Telephone #7, 1904 100-Digit Dial, 1983, $45-50.

Trophy Series
1957-1988

Sailfish, 1957. $15-20. Muskie, 1971. $23-28. Sturgeon (belongs to Organization series pg. 70), 1980, $15-20. Trout Unlimited, 1977, $15-20.

Fish Hall of Fame. Largemouth Bass, 1973, $20-25. Bluegill, 1974, $20-25. Rainbow Trout, 1975, $15-20. Salmon Coho, 1976, $20-25.

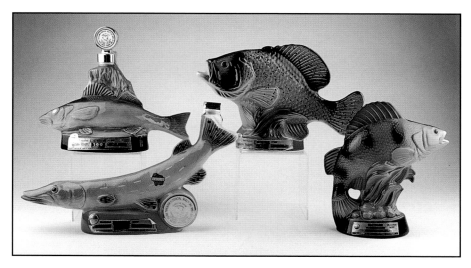

Fishing Hall of Fame. Walleye Pike, 1977, $22-27. Northern Pike, 1978, $20-25. Crappie, 1979, $20-25. Pretty Perch, 1980, $18-23.

Catfish, 1981, $35-40.
Muskie "Fishing Hall of
Fame," 1983, $32-37.
Walleye, 1987, $20-25.

Setter, 1958. The smaller one on the right may be a counterfeit. It's about 92 percent of the size of the larger one, a different color, and lighter in weight. A regular bottle was probably used as a mold to create smaller counterfeit. Original, $20-25.

Duck, 1957. $20-25

Ram with thermometer, 1958. $40-45

Pheasant, 1960. $12-20

Horses, Black, Brown, and Grey. 1961-62, $20-25. 1966-68, $15-20.

Green fox, 1965-67. $12-17

Doe, 1963 and 1967, with different colors. $15-20

Eagle, 1966-68. $10-15

Three cats. Burmese, Siamese, and Tabby, 1967. $15-20

Robin, 1969, $8-12. Woodpecker, 1969, $8-12.

Cardinal, female, 1973, $12-15. Cardinal, male, 1968, $22-25.
Blue Jay, 1969, $8-12.

Poodles, grey and white, 1970. $8-12

Rabbit, 1971. $12-17

Jackelope, 1971.
$12-17.

Tiffiny, 1973. Mascot of National Association of
Jim Beam Bottle & Specialties Clubs. $14-18

Appaloosa, 1974. $10-15

Great Dane, 1976, $12-18. St. Bernard, 1979, $30-35.

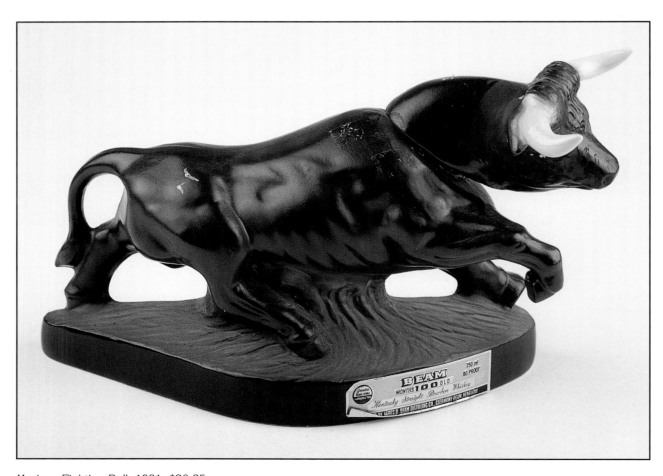

Mexican Fighting Bull, 1981. $20-25

Mare and Foal, "For the Love of a Horse," 1982, $45-50. Mare and Foal, "Oh! Kentucky," 1982, $75-80.

Harp seals, 1986. $18-22

Armadillo, 1981. $15-20

Eagle, 1985. $25-30

Left: Duck Decoy, 1988. $40-45
Right: Rare duck decoy bottle from the Peabody Hotel. $150

Pewter Horses, 1986. $25-30

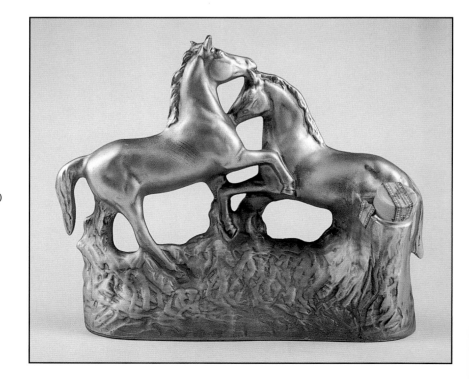

Glass Decanters

Beam's glass decanters represent a branch of collecting all their own. The earliest decorative Beam bottles were clear glass bottles, whose popularity with customers led the way for ceramic bottle designs. As ceramic bottles caught on, Beam continued to offer a wonderful assortment of clear and colored glass in some very elaborate designs.

Many of the glass bottles were made by the famous Wheaton Glass Company of Millville, New Jersey.

Crystal Glass Series

1959-1976

Royal Crystal, 1959, $5.

Teal Blue, 1973, $25-30. Genie blue, smoked without handle, 1964, $45-50.

Crystal Pressed bottles, 1966-1974. Colors include black, blue, clear (contained Bourbon, Vodka, or Scotch) emerald (contained Borbon or Brandy), marbelized grey, opaline, ruby, white, and amber. $5 each

Crystal Sunburst, 1974-75. Colors include amber, azure blue, black, bronze, blue, gold, green, red, smoke. $4 each.

Crystal Sunburst bottles. Dark Eyes Vodka, and the "Poor Man's Speckled Beauty", 1975. $30-35 each.

Crystal Sunburst bottles with Trave labels containing flavored liquors, 1975. Amaretto, Chocolomi, Espresso, and Jubilee. $3 each.

Glass Series
1940-1986

Pins. Gold top, amber, $18-22, and clear, $2-5. White Ten Pin, 1980, $5-10. White top, $5-10. These came with various aged liquors.

Wood top pins, 1940-52. Fifth bottle with eight years and six years, $10-30; pint bottle, $10-15.

Cocktail shaker, 1953-54, $5-10. With "Chateaux Martini" label, $45-50. This is one of the first decorative Jim Beam decanters offered.

Royal Reserve, 1953, $5-10. Another Royal Reserve decanter was produced in 1976. Zimmerman's glass, 1969, $8-12.

Pyrex

The Corning Glass Company of Corning, N.Y. produced several Pyrex decanters for Beam, starting in 1954. These reusable decanters were sold in liquor stores.

Pyrex Coffee Warmers. With gold handle, 1956, $8-12. Handle adds $2-3 in value. Without handle, black, gold, green, red, or white, $8-12.

Ducks and Geese, 1955, $3-8. Fiesta Bowl, 1970, $10-20.

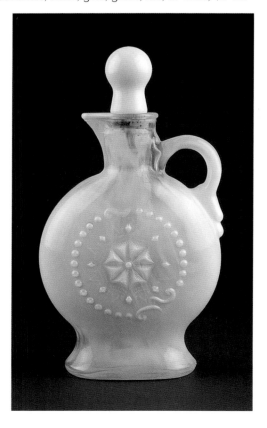

Far left: Royal Opal, 1957. $5-10

Left: Royal Emperor, 1958, $3

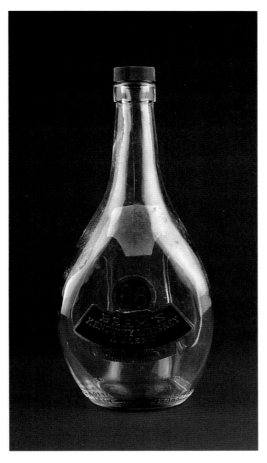

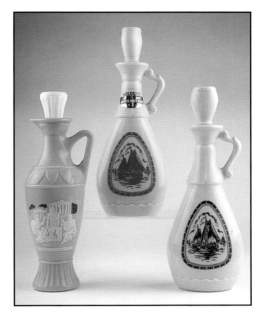

Grecian, 1961, $3. Delft rose, 1963, $3. Delft blue, 1963, $5.

Tall Pinch bottle, 1959, $100. Also released in 1956, $150; 1966, $25; 1968-78, $5-10

Olympian, 1960, $2. Olympic, 1971, $4. Oriental Jade, 1972, $4.

Cleopatra, 1962. Rust, $1-5, and Yellow, $10-15. Mark Anthony, 1962, $15-20. Mark Anthony was shown without Cleopatra on some bottles because at the time some states restricted the sale of liquor with pictures of women.

Music-box bottles. Dancing Scott, Tall, 1964, $20-25. Dancing Scot, Short, 1963, $60-65. Dancing Couple, 1964, $150-175.

Portola Trek and Powell Expedition, 1969, $5 each.

Cameo Blue, 1965. $2

Harvey Hotel, 1969, $15-20. Herre Brothers, (belongs to Customer Specialty series), 1972, $25-30. Humbolt Country Fair, 1970, $12-17.

Beatty Wild Burro Races, 1970. $10-15

California Derby, 1971, $5-10. Go-with glasses showing derby winners, $1-2 each. Complete set $50.

Crispus Attucks, 1976. Biography of the Revolutionary War hero on back. $3-8

Cannon, 1970. Vodka Dark Eyes in darker bottle, or bourbon. $2-5

Rockwell series, Saturday Evening Post covers, 1975. Elect Casey, Ye Pipe and Bowl, Pioneers, Home Coming, Benjamin Franklin, Game Called. $4-10 each.

Choice, 1976. Gold and silver
(not shown), $4-8 each.

Spey Royal, 1976. $4-8

Ruby, 1980, $8-12.

Jim Beam 200th Anniversary bottle,
1795-1995. $30-35 with box.

Collector Glass Series
1966-1983

Perhaps the most common of the Beam decanters, the Collector's Edition Decanters were available in the retail market from 1966 to 1986. A set of pint-size decanters was introduced each year, known as a volume; each volume had from three to eight decanters sporting a specific artistic theme. The bottles featured artwork from painters of all eras, and often included biographical information on the other side. Earlier volumes also included matching cups.

From an investment standpoint, the bottles have not increased much in value. From a collector's standpoint, it is certainly a challenge to hunt them all down, and a fascinating study of art history along the way!

James Lockhart

Many of the later Collector's Edition bottles feature detailed paintings of wildlife; this is the artwork of esteemed painter James Lockhart. The artist has come to many conventions to sign his bottles.

Collector's Edition, Volume #2, 1967. Night Watch, The Jester, Georg Gisze, and Man on Horse, $3-6 each. Soldier and Girl and Nurse and Child, $4-7 each.

Collector's Edition, Volume #3, 1968. The Buffalo Hunt, American Gothic, Hauling in the Gill Net, The Scout, $3-6 each.

Collector's Edition, Volume #1, 1966. Aristide Bruant, Artist, Laughing Cavalier, Mardi Gras, $3-6 each. Blue Boy, and On the Terrace, $5-8 each. Go-with glasses, $1-2 each.

Collector's Edition, Volume #3, 1968. The Kentuckian, Whistler's Mother, On the Trail, Indian Maiden, $3-6 each.

Collector's Edition, Volume #4, 1969. Emile Zola, Fruit Basket, Zouave, Guitarist, $4 each.

Collector's Edition, Volume #4, 1969. The Balcony, Sunflowers, The Judge, Boy with Cherries, $4 each.

Collector's Edition, Volume #5, 1970. Boating Party, Titus Writing Desk, Gare St. Lazare, Au Cafe, Jewish Bride, Old Peasant, $3 each.

Collector's Edition, Volume #6, 1971. Charles I, Boy with Flute, Merry Lute Player. $3 each.

Collector's Edition, Volume #7, 1972. Maidservant, Bag Piper, Prince Carlos. $3 each.

Collector's Edition, Volume #8, 1973.
Beethhoven, Chopin, Mozart. $3 each.

Collector's Edition, Volume #9, 1974. Cardinal,
Woodcock, Pheasant. $3 each.

Collector's Edition, Volume #11, 1976. Anatelope, Bighorn, Chipmunk. $5-8 each.

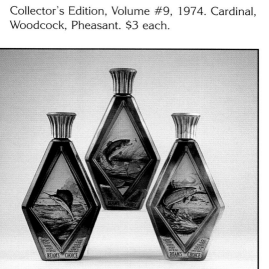

Collector's Edition, Volume #10, 1975. Sailfish,
Bass, Trout. $4-7 each.

Collector's Edition, Volume #12, 1977. Irish
Setter, German Shorthaired Pointer, Labrador
Retriever, Springer Spaniel. $4-6 each.

Collector's Edition, Volume #14, 1978. Cottontail Rabbit, Red fox, Raccoon, Mule Deer. $5-8 each.

Collector's Edition, Volume #16, 1980. Redhead, mallard, canvasback, $5-8 each.

Collector's Edition, Volume #15, 1979. Paintings by Frederick Remington (1861-1909). Biography of artist and information about the paintings on back of bottles. Lt. S.C. Robertson, The Cowboy, and Indian Trapper. $5-8 each.

Collector's Edition, Volume #17, 1981. Horned Owl, Great Elk, Pintail Duck. $5-8 each.

Collector's Edition, Volume #18, 1982. Whitetail Deer, Grey Fox, Cardinal. $5-8 each.

Collector's Edition, Volume #19 1983: Scarlet Tanger, Whitetail Deer, Wood Duck. $5-8 each.

Collector's Edition, Volume #21, 1985 (Duck Stamp Series).
Green-Wing Teal, Mallard, Widgeon, $8-11 each.

Collector's Edition, Volume #20, 1984 (Duck Stamp Series).
Pintail, Canvasback, Ruddy, $5-10 each.

Collector's Edition, Volume #22, 1986 (Duck Stamp Series).
Hooded Merganser, Cinnamon Teal, Ross Geese, $4-9.

Convention Glass

Among the limited edition bottles and go-withs available at each convention, glass bottles were often offered as well. Usually, there were four of these bottles per convention, containing Bourbon, Vodka, Gin, and Scotch. The 1983 St. Louis covention bottle set had five bottles, as it included brandy, tequila, and Canadian whiskey in addition to the other four. The glass convention giveaways listed below, and examples are illustrated with the ceramic convention bottles, as noted.

- 8th Convention, 1978: Chicago, Illinois
  Bourbon, Gin, Scotch, Vodka
  See example on page 27

- 9th Convention, 1979: Houston, Texas
  Bourbon, Gin, Scotch, Vodka
  See example on page 27

- 10th Convention, 1980: Norfolk, Virginia
  Bourbon, Gin, Scotch, Vodka
  See example on page 27

- 11th Convention, 1981: Las Vegas, Nevada
  Bourbon, Gin, Scotch, Vodka
  See example on page 27

- 12th Convention, 1982: New Orleans, Louisiana
  Bourbon, Gin, Scotch, Vodka

- 13th Convention, 1983: St. Louis, Missouri
  Bourbon, Brandy, Gin, Scotch, Vodka, Tequila, Canadian Whiskey

- 14th Convention, 1984: Hollywood, Florida
  Bourbon, Gin, Scotch, Vodka
  See example on page 28

Houston Convention bottle, 1979. Signed by Angelo Aggelopoulos and J.J. McShane. Without signature, $3. Much more valuable with signatures.

Decanters to Go

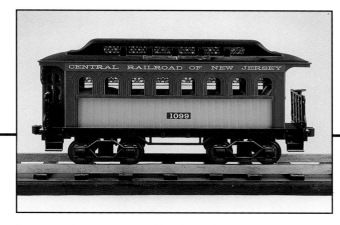

Grant set: Passenger car, 1981. $35-40

This section covers decanters modeled after vehicles of all kinds, including cars, trucks, trains—even a space shuttle. These marvelous decanters represent the most popular branch of Beam bottle collecting, and as a group seem to be commanding the highest prices. The Train Series is an elegant group of decanters, featuring four different sets. The Wheel Series offers the broadest range of vehicles, although many belong to other series, including Convention, Customer Specialty, and Regal Special. Identifying vehicle decanters can be tricky, as so many models and variations were produced over the years. The color alone can mean the difference of hundreds of dollars between two otherwise identical models.

Train Series

1979-1990

Grant set: Baggage, 1981. $35-40

Grant set: Engine, 1980, $65-70. Coal Tender, $55-65. Shown with homemade track.

Grant set: Observation car, 1985. $50-55

Grant set: Caboose, 1980. $45-50

Grant set: Dining car, 1982. $65-70

Turner set: Engine, 1982, $95-100. Not shown: wood tender, $45-50.
Shown with genuine track, $15-20 per piece.

Turner set: Tank car, 1983. $45-50

Turner set: Brown boxcar, 1983. $45-50

Turner set: Log car, 1984. $55-65

Turner set: Lumber car, 1986. $45-50

Turner set: Caboose, 1989. $85-90

Water Towers. The dark brown tower (right) is a decanter, while the light brown one (left) is not. $45-50

136

General train set: Engine, 1986, $95-100. Wood tender, 1988, $120-125.

General train set: Flat car, 1988. $75-80

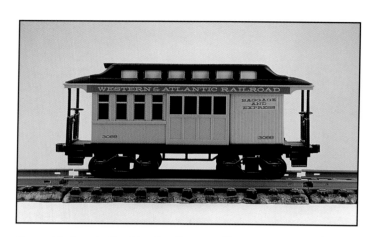

General train set: Combination Baggage/Express car, 1988. $45-50

General train set: Grey caboose, 1988. $65-70

Casey Jones set: Engine with tender, 1989. $40-45

Casey Jones set: Box Car, 1990, $30-35. Tank car, 1990, $40-45. Caboose, 1989, $20-25.
Track, three pieces, 1990, $5-10 each. Bumper, $5-10 each.

Wheel Series

1972-1992

To help with identification, included here are vehicle decanters from the Convention Series, Customer Specialty Series, and The Regal Special Series.

Chevrolet

Bel Air

'57 Chevy Belair, hardtop. Black, 1987, $80-90. Turquoise and white, 1987, $65-75. Sierra Gold special edition, available to members attending the 1988 district meeting, $100-110. The '57 Bel Air hardtop was also offered in dark blue, and was originally sold in Pennsylvania, $75.

'57 Chevy Bel Air hardtop, yellow hotrod, 1988. $100-110

'57 Chevy Bel Air convertible. Blue special edition, 1990, $110-120. Cream special edition, 1990, $100-110. These two cars were offered as his and her giveaways for the 20th convention in Kissimmee, Florida. Black, 1990, $70-80. Red, 1990, $90-100. Turquoise and white, 1991, $55-65. White special edition (not shown), 1992, $500. A special silver one-of-a-kind is owned by Art & Judy Turner.

Camaro

'69 Camaro hardtop. Orange Hugger, 1988, $60-70. Yellow Pennsylvania issue, 1988, $60-70. Blue and white top, 1988, $60-70. Blue and beige top, $60-70. Not shown: Green special edition, 1988—150 were sold through the IAJBB&SC.

'69 Camaro convertible. Orange and white pace car, 1988, $110-120. Burgundy special edition, 1989, $110-120. Silver special edition, 1989, $115-125. These two were his (silver) and hers (burgundy) giveaways for the 19th convention in Kansas City.

Corvette

'78 Corvette. White, 1985, $70-80. Yellow, 1985, $65-75. Black and silver pace car, 1987, $250+. Black, 1984, $125-135. Red, 1984, $70-80.

'63 Stingray. Black Pennsylvania issue, 1988, $95-105. Blue New York issue, 1989, $100-110.

'63 Stingray. Red, 1987, $85-95. Silver, 1987, $75-85. Not shown: Green, 1992, $350-plus, made for club members in a limited edition of 700.

'84 Corvette, 1988. Red, $75-85. White, $55-65. Black Western edition, $95-105. Bronze special edition, $105-115. Gold special edition, $90-100. The bronze and gold special editions were available at the 1989 District meeting.

'55 Corvette. Black special edition, 1990, $100-120. Copper/bronze, 1989, $100-120. Red special edition, 1990, $115-125. The black and the red models were only available at the 1990 District meeting.

'54 Corvette, blue, 1989, $150-160. Not pictured: '53 Corvette, white, 1989, $125-150.

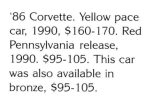

'86 Corvette. Yellow pace car, 1990, $160-170. Red Pennsylvania release, 1990. $95-105. This car was also available in bronze, $95-105.

'57 Corvette. Black, 1991, $70-80. Blue special edition, 1991, $520-plus. White with Angelo's Liquors sticker, 1991, $165-175. Red with Angelo's Liquors sticker, 1991, $250-275. Copper special edition, 1991, $120-130. Turquoise special edition, 1991, $180-190. The copper and turquoise cars were available to members attending the 1991 District meeting.

'68 Corvette. Maroon, 1992, $50-60. White with Angelo's Liquors sticker, $50-100. Blue, 1992, $60-70. Green special edition, $170-180. Yellow special edition, 1992, $170-180. The green and yellow cars were available to members at the 1992 converntion. Red with Angelo's Liquors sticker, 1992, $90-100. Not shown: Black, $850-plus. Bronzestone special edition,1992, $1,400-plus. Silverstone special edition, 1992, $2,500-plus.

Cadillac

'59 Cadillac convertible. Light Green, 1992, $100-120. Blue, 1992, $150-160. Pink, 1992, $55-65. White, 1992, $260-275. Black, 1992, $300-325.

Ford

1913 Ford Model T. Black, 1974, $45-50. Green, 1974, $45-50.

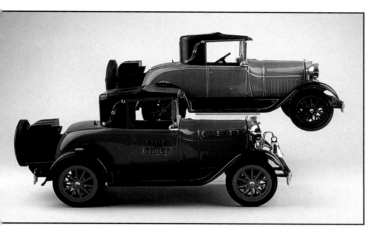

'28 Model A. Green coupe, 1980, $65-70. Fire Chief, 1981, $95-100. Not shown: Black salesman award, 1981, $800-plus. Yellow salesman award, 1981, $500-600-plus.

'28-29 Model A pickup truck, special release for Parkwood Supply, 1984, $100-125. A plain model ($200-plus) was released, along with three other special releases for Angelo's Liquors ($250), Palumbo Distributing ($500), and Western Distributing ($700).

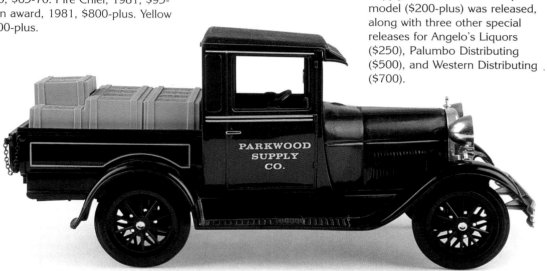

1903 Ford Model A. Black, 1978, $50-55. Red, 1979, $45-50.

'29 Phaeton. Green, 1982, $65-70. Blue police car, 1982, $90-100. Not shown: Yellow police car, 1983, $400.

'29 Woodie Delivery Wagon, 1984, $65-75.

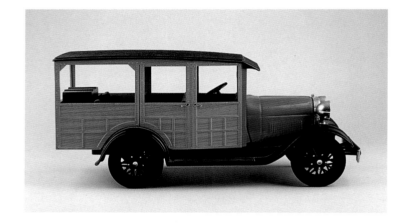

'29 Delivery Wagon, 1984. Black special edition, $95-105. Green special edition, $95-105. These were sold through the IAJBB&SC.

'35 Pickup Truck, $65-70. Police tow truck, 1987, $75-80. Angelo's Liquors, 1987, $75-80.

'34 Roadster. Cream, special Pennsylvania release, 1990, $90-95. Fire Chief, 1988, $65-70.

Thunderbird

'56 Thunderbird. Grey, 1986, $95-100. Yellow, 1986, $105-115. Not shown: Black, 1986, $95-100. Blue Pennsylvania release, 1986, $120-125. Green, 1986, $95-100.

Mustang

'64 Mustang, 1986. Red, $90-95. White, $75-80. Black Florida release, $125-130.

Mercedes

1974 Mercedes. Gold, Angelo's, 1987, $50-55. Mocha special edition (available at 1974 district meeting), 1987, $50-55. Red, 1986, $50-55. Silver, produced for Australia, 1987, $100-105. White, 1986, $65-70. Not shown: Blue, 1987, $45-50. Green, 1987, $45-50, Sand Beige, Pennsylvania release, 1987, $50-55.

Fire and Police Vehicles

The '28 Fire Chief Car (1981), '29 Police Car (1982), '34 Fire Chief (1988), '35 Police Tow Truck (1987) appear with the Ford vehicles on page 145.

Mississippi Fire Truck Pumper, 1978. $45-50

1917 Mack Fire Truck, 1982. $95-100

1930 Model A Fire Truck, 1983, $150-200.

1931 Model A Paddy Wagon, 1983, $95-100. 1931 Model A Ambulance, 1985, $65-70.

1934 Fire Truck Pumper, 1987, $85-90.

Chevy Troopers. Blue special edition, 1992, $70-80. Grey special edition, 1992, $60-70. White, 1992, $30-40.

1934 Roadster Patrol Cars. White, 1989, $100-110. Yellow special edition, 1989, $125-130.

Other Vehicles

1904 Oldsmobile, 1972. $50

Jewel Tea Wagon, 1974. $65-75

Harold's Covered Wagon, 1974. $30-35

Volkswagon, 1973. Blue,
$45-50. Red, $45-50.

Bobby Unser's #48
Olsonite, 1975. $45-50

Vendome Wagon,
1975. $35-40

1907 Thomas Flyer. Blue, 1976, $45. Ivory, 1976, $45.

1914 Stutz Bearcat, 1977. Grey, $40. Yellow, $40.

Circus Wagon, 1979. Horse sold seperately. $23-28

1934 Duesenburgs. Dark Blue special edition, 1982, $100-110. Light Blue, 1981, $100-110. Not shown: White "Great Race", 1984, $1,800-plus.

1935 Duesenburg convertible. Maroon and cream, 1983, $140-150.
Not shown: Maroon and grey, special edition, 1983, $250-260.

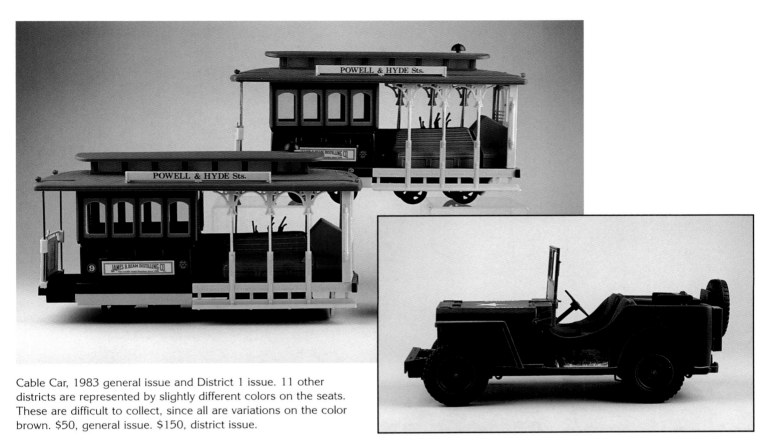

Cable Car, 1983 general issue and District 1 issue. 11 other districts are represented by slightly different colors on the seats. These are difficult to collect, since all are variations on the color brown. $50, general issue. $150, district issue.

Army Jeep, 1986. $45-50

Golf Cart, 1986. $45-50

Bass Boat with Trailer, 1987. $35-40

Semi-tractor trailer, 18-wheelers: Yellow special edition ("hers" convention offer), 1991, $65-70. White, 1991, $55-60. Also, a special edition in gold (not shown), $2,500; silver special edition, $1,500; orange special edition, $65-70. Other tractor trailers made include "Food for Less" and Angelo's Liquors, both of which appear in the Customer Specialty section.

Semi-Tractor Trailer, Food for Less. $400

Semi-tractor trailer, 18-wheeler: Angelo's Liquors, bronze & red, 1991, $70-75. Angelo's truck in beige (not shown), $75-80.

1970 Dodge Challengers. Blue special edition, 1991, $175-185. Yellow hotrod, 1992, $50-60. Lime green special edition, 1992, $115-125. Plum, 1991, $60-70. Not shown: Red, 1992, $500+.

Sand and gravel dump truck, 1992. $45-50

Odds and Ends

Here are some other Beam bottles you may encounter in the marketplace.

Black Canasta. "The Bottle that Wasn't" on tag, describing how Beam originally rejected this design in 1957 and sold it to Peyton's Distillery. The bottle can be laid on its back and used for dealing cards. $5-10

Oil lamp, Beam Black Label, 1981. This is not a decanter. $20-25

Bronte Jug, plain and two-tone: 12-ounce, $5-7. 24-ounce, $7-9. There were also pedestals made to display these crocks.

Corked bottles signed C. Miller, with Jim Beam corks, to double as coffee warmers. Referred to by collectors as "carafes." 1957. Come in a variety of colors and patterns. $35-40

Beameister Crock, 1972-77, twelve different colors, $3-6 each.

A Word About Wade

Jim Beam decanters were, for the most part, produced by Regal China up until 1992. When the company ceased operations at that time, The IAJBB&SC approached Wade Ceramics, Ltd., Stoke-on-Trent, England, about producing their 1993 convention bottle. The bottle was a tremendous success, and Wade continued to produce their convention bottles in the years that followed, along with many go-with items and collector promotions (see page 31 for examples of these convention designs).

In 1996, the International Wade Collectors Club and the IAJBB&SC pooled their efforts and made membership available to one another. For the last few years the conventions have coincided so collectors from both clubs can enjoy the wonderful items offered by Wade.

Bibliography

Cembura, Al, and Avery, Constance. *Jim Beam Bottles: 1971/72 Identification and Price Guide.* Berkely: Cembura and Avery Publishers, 1971.

Cembura, Al, and Avery, Constance. *Jim Beam Bottles: 1972/73 Identification and Price Guide.* Berkely: Cembura and Avery Publishers, 1971.

Honeyman, Betty, ed., and The International Association of Jim Beam Bottle and Specialties Clubs. *Jim Beam Bottles: A Pictorial Guide.* Dallas: Taylor Publishing Co, 1982.

Montague, H.F. *Montague's Modern Bottle Identification and Price Guide.* Overland Park: Montague Enterprises, 1984.